D1361608

Four Roses

BOURBON

Four Roses®

THE RETURN OF A WHISKEY LEGEND

AL YOUNG

BUTLER BOOKS

LOUISVILLE

DEDICATION

This book is dedicated to a true brand champion and friend, Teruyuki Daino, who always wanted to know more about Four Roses.

In doing so, he inspired me to take on the delightful and enlightening task of researching the company archives and outside sources, along with talking to many of the people who have had a hand in developing the brand into what it has become today. I have also included some photographs, where available, of some of the brand's highlights over more than 125 years – through some of the most interesting, remarkable and turbulent times in the history of the United States.

ACKNOWLEDGMENTS

I first came here in 1982 as a shift supervisor with Joseph E. Seagram & Sons, Inc., from the Calvert Distillery on 7th Street Road in Louisville, Kentucky. Because of this step in my career, it was literally "love at first sight" that led me to want to know more about the history of our main building and, later, the Four Roses brand.

It would have been almost impossible to complete this book without the help of many people who gave of their time and resources to make this happen.

First, I would like to especially thank Dr. Lawrence M. Jones; Mrs. Elizabeth Jones LeBus (Missy) Lang; the late Lawrence Jones (Larry) Middleton and Roland Jones for giving me access to family papers and writings that revealed interesting tidbits about their colorful family heritage.

Along with everything else, enthusiasm and perseverance are reasons enough to thank my supervisor, Ms. Patty Holland, Director, Sales and Marketing, for her positive attitude and devotion to the project. Her determination to see it completed kept it moving forward at all times.

To my colleagues, former Master Distiller Jim Rutledge and Sr. Marketing Manager Julie Gorham at the Four Roses Distillery, and Director of our Warehouse Bottling Facility at Cox's Creek, Corey Ballard, my continuing thanks for the information that you willingly shared with me for the writing of this book.

I am also thankful to: Dr. Lindsey Apple (Ret.), History Department, Georgetown College, Georgetown, Kentucky; the late Dr. Samuel W. Thomas, regional writer; and Mike Veach, Associate Curator of Special Collections, The Filson Historical Society, both in Louisville, for sharing with me some of their writing organizational skills and informational resources for this work.

Extremely special thanks must also go to Tim Hellige, Gary Sloboda, Mark Miller and Matt Kamer for providing me with point-in-time advice at every step of the way during the editing and pre-publication process. It is they who took a simple manuscript and made it live.

Finally, I owe my undying gratitude to my wife, Gretchen. From the beginning, it was she who always supported me and successfully came to understand the importance that I gave to this work on many Saturdays and Sundays over the past few years. Her encouragement fueled the passion for me to finish this story about Four Roses.

- A. Young

INTRODUCTION

The Four Roses story is one filled with adventure and romance, with a cast of colorful characters any fiction writer would die for. A father and son enamored of the Southern cause during the American Civil War; another son, a Confederate Colonel who dies defending Atlanta; and then his sons who would successfully turn the family business into one of the last family-owned whiskey brands in the United States; a whiskey magnate who would alter the brand's composition within the United States and drive it to be a "bottom shelf" brand; and, finally, a passionate and determined Master Distiller who would never give in until Four Roses regained the prominence it once had with the American public.

Larger than life, these people have all contributed to the brand's current place and stature in the world, which includes such countries as Austria, the Czech Republic, France, Germany, Italy, Japan, the Netherlands, Spain, Switzerland, the United Kingdom and, of course, once again the United States.

It is also a story about the passion and single-mindedness that drives those of us here at Four Roses to make unique, exceptionally fine Bourbons from 10 Bourbon recipes according to the traditions and time-proven methods at both our distillery in Lawrenceburg, Kentucky and our Warehouse & Bottling Facility in Cox's Creek, Kentucky.

So, if this is your first taste of "the Four Roses Story," or even if you've known about it for some time, you might be saying to yourself, "What is he talking about?" Well, come along and join me as we take a look at the Four Roses brand's ever-evolving history and what has become a truly remarkably story of the return of a whiskey legend.

© 2016 Four Roses Distillery LLC

Third Edition

All Rights Reserved.

No part of this book may be reproduced or transmitted
in any form or by any means, electronic or mechanical,
including photocopying or recording, or by any
information storage and retrieval system, without
permission in writing from the author or his assigns.

ISBN 978-1-935497-29-5

Printed in Canada

Book and Cover Design by
Bandy Carroll Hellige
Louisville, Kentucky

Published by:

Butler Books
P.O. Box 7311
Louisville, KY 40257
(502) 897–9393
Fax (502) 897–9797
www.butlerbooks.com

Contents

THE JONES FAMILY TREE

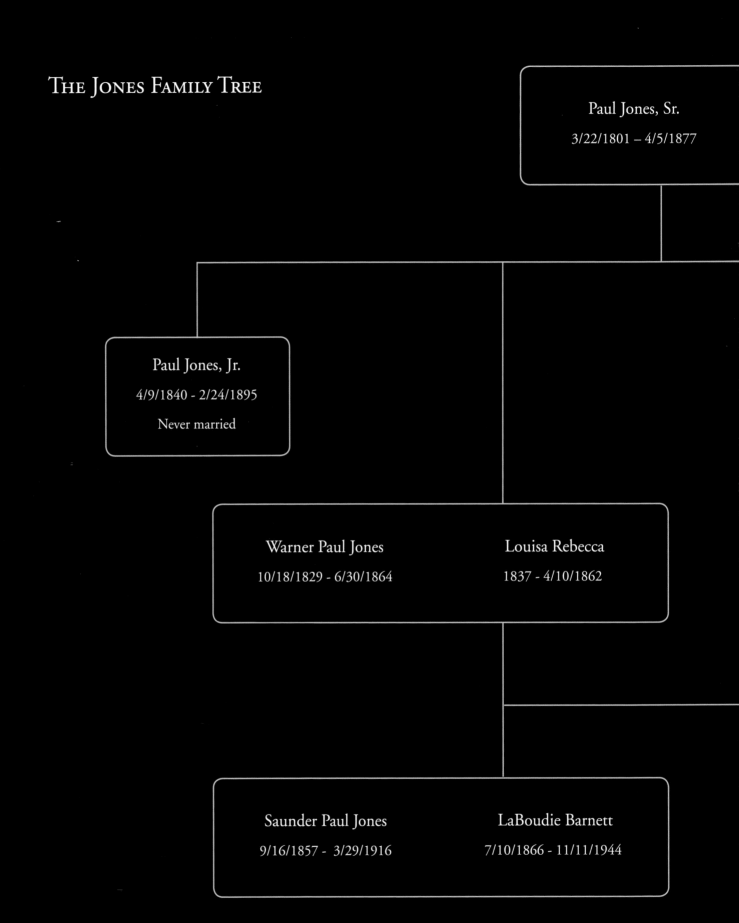

Paul Jones, Sr.

3/22/1801 – 4/5/1877

Paul Jones, Jr.

4/9/1840 - 2/24/1895

Never married

Warner Paul Jones

10/18/1829 - 6/30/1864

Louisa Rebecca

1837 - 4/10/1862

Saunder Paul Jones

9/16/1857 - 3/29/1916

LaBoudie Barnett

7/10/1866 - 11/11/1944

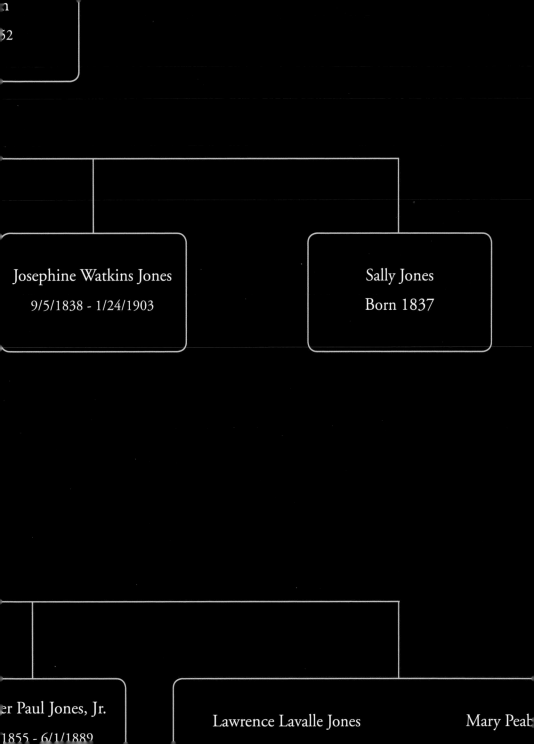

52

Josephine Watkins Jones

9/5/1838 - 1/24/1903

Sally Jones

Born 1837

er Paul Jones, Jr.

1855 - 6/1/1889

Lawrence Lavalle Jones

Mary Peab

CHAPTER ONE:

The Start of Something Beautiful. 1840-1883

Keeping up with the Joneses

According to family papers, the Jones family that would later become so influential in the whiskey business could trace its ancestry back to 17th century England before coming to the colonies to settle in Lynchburg, Virginia. Their main source of business for some years was operating a coach line between Lynchburg and New York City.

It is further recorded that one Paul Jones, Sr. married Mary Walton in 1828. Together they would have two daughters and two sons. The two boys, Paul, Jr. and Warner Paul, would, as we shall discover, soon have a lasting impact on the family's future whiskey business and, of course, the world of Bourbon.

By the 1840s, the winds of war and secession were being fanned by young, hot-headed southern state senators in the Congress of the United States. Even a highly influential Kentuckian by the name of Henry Clay, also known as the "Great Compromiser," could not stop it. This is the same guy that was rumored to have enjoyed his whiskey so much that he would jump up on (and dance the length of) the banquet table at "Ashland," his estate in Lexington, Kentucky. How inspiring that must have been.

Did you know?

Henry Clay's drink of choice was Old Crow. This same whiskey was also the favorite of Union General U.S. Grant. It is not known for sure, but President Abraham Lincoln was rumored to have been thinking about ordering some for the rest of his generals as a way to get them to fight like Grant.

The Civil War

As the war drew closer, Paul, Sr., Paul, Jr., and Warner Paul, got caught up in the fervor of "Southern Rights" to the point that they all invested in Confederate war bonds to finance the rebels. Warner Paul, full of angst for "the cause," went so far as to enlist in the 33rd regiment of Tennessee Volunteers, Confederate States of America after the war broke out. It can only be guessed that both his father and brother fell right in there with him.

Their story has a Kentucky connection in that this particular part of the Confederate Army would be under the command of General Braxton Bragg, directed by General Kirby Smith, as part of the rebels' attempt to invade and conquer this decidedly neutral and strategically important border state.

This part of the rebel army, with newly promoted Colonel Warner Paul Jones, would invade from Northern Tennessee and link up with Kirby's command coming east from the Bardstown area. It is interesting to note that they would have passed by our current Human Resources Manager Jeanette Pfalzer's farm on Paxton Road, close by our current distillery. She has heard it said that there is proof that the highest part of the land was used as a Confederate lookout post during 1862.

It is more than likely that they would have marched down to what is now known as Bonds Mill Road to link up with the Confederate Army coming in from Southern Kentucky. Their hopes were to invade Frankfort, take over the government, and then move on to Louisville to take control of the Ohio River with its rich river traffic.

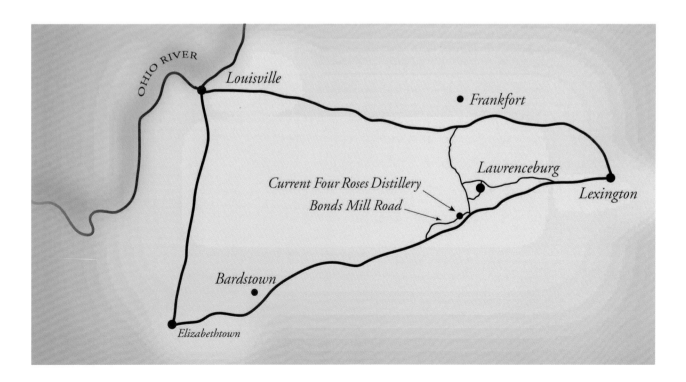

President Abraham Lincoln

As a side note, it is probably worth mentioning that the so-called invasion of Kentucky by the rebels could also have been what we may call a sort of "rebel shopping trip" for badly needed raw materials to continue the war. With their copper mines in the south now under federal control, they had to depend on blockade runners to provide them with the percussion caps made out of thin sheets of this metal or look for other sources for it. Since almost every farm in this area had a small copper still to make either whiskey or cider, it was only natural to collect them, roll them flat and make what was needed.

If we look at things the way they were in that part of Kentucky in 1862, we find it hard to believe that both armies from the North and South, with no plans for engagement, literally blundered into each other and fought what is now known as "The Battle of Perryville." There are a lot of published accounts of the battle that are better, and longer, than this one but when it was over the facts remain the same. Nobody really won. The rebels accounted for 510 dead, 2,635 wounded while the Union said 845 of theirs were dead and 2,851 were wounded.

Colonel Warner Paul Jones and the 33rd Tennessee had given a good showing throughout the battle by taking the high ground and returning fire on the enemy to cover the retreat. In Jones' family copies of CSA dispatches, he would be commended for his "bravery and warrior-like abilities."

While President Abraham Lincoln was happy that "Above all else, we must have Kentucky" had held true, he was dismayed that the Confederate Army had been allowed to escape back into Tennessee and probably knew that the war would drag on even longer as a result of it.

Commander Nathan Bedford Forrest

Getting back to our story, Colonel Jones had suffered a personal tragedy during the same year when his wife died in Vicksburg, Mississippi. They'd had three sons who were now entrusted to the care of the colonel's sister and her husband in the eastern part of Missouri.

It was the separation from his children that led the colonel to request a transfer from the regiment to form an independent cavalry company in western Tennessee under the command of the legendary Commander Nathan Bedford Forrest, who some in the Union Army believed was the devil himself. This change would place Colonel Jones closer to his children whom he missed desperately and wanted to have a hand in raising.

Now here is the important part, since he was such a good officer and full of patriotic verve for the cause, they honored his request. There was, of course, one small problem with all of this. Manpower in western Tennessee was simply not available to form any kind of military force for either side back then. With this in mind, the Colonel then asked to go back to his old regiment, now on its way to Atlanta. His request was granted and he joined them as they headed south into Georgia.

Colonel Warner Paul Jones and his late wife's three sons were named Warner, Jr., Saunders Paul and Lawrence Lavalle. They were 8, 6 and 4 years old, respectively, when they lived with their aunt in Missouri. Little did they know what was about to happen to them as their father and his regiment headed for Atlanta.

You know, life is full of a lot of "what-ifs?" but it might have been a different outcome for the family if Colonel Jones would have stayed in western Tennessee. Maybe all of them would have rubbed elbows with some older rebels like the outlaw William Quantrill and his murderous guerillas, or even with the notorious bank and train robbers, Frank and Jesse James. Perhaps the boys (who all grew up to be refined Southern gentlemen) could have become the recipients of a lack of up-bringing that would have changed forever the course of their involvement with Four Roses.

Sadly, it was recorded that Colonel Warner Paul Jones was killed by a Yankee sharpshooter (sniper) on Kennesaw Mountain while on an early morning reconnaissance mission as the Yankees advanced on the city. He was both lauded and praised for his leadership and soldiering abilities in official documents still in the possession of Dr. Lawrence Jones, currently residing in Louisville. Another descendant still has the regiment's battle flag as well.

There is an interesting story about the Jones family and their times in the writings of Katherine Jones Smith, the granddaughter of one of the Colonel's sons, Lawrence Lavalle Jones.

"It was in the battle of Atlanta that Confederate Colonel Warner Paul Jones lost his life and left his three small sons fatherless to live with their uncle. The most vivid memory Granddaddy had of the Civil War was when the Yankees marched into Atlanta. It was a great day of woe and one long to be remembered by small Lawrence. That morning, when the three little boys and their two cousins were playing in the yard, they spied to their horror a group of Yankee soldiers headed full march for their house. Needless to say they were petrified. In their small minds, they had built up a horrible legend about Yankee soldiers from hearing conversations of the grownups. Their first impulse was to hide and they obeyed it. They ran speedily to the large bed and dived underneath it into the wonderful haven that it offered. Little Lawrence, being the youngest, was the last to get under the bed and, since there was only a minute bit of room remaining, he let his two small legs protrude out from under the coverlet.

When the soldiers stomped noisily into the bedroom, a burly Yankee spied the two legs and dragged the hiding child into the open. Seeing a quaking child of about five in front of him, he was amused. He kindly told my grandfather not to be afraid and, through his kindness, he taught a small frightened southern boy that northerners weren't such terrible monsters after all."

It is interesting to note that wartime in these early days created its own taxation problems for the whiskey industry when the government's needs for money were the greatest. For example, a 7-cent tax a gallon on whiskey caused what was called the "Whiskey Rebellion," in an attempt to pay off war debts in 1792.

During the Civil War, the tax went to $2 a gallon, although in 1867, a government economist recommended that the tax be cut to 50 cents. As he stated, "Any higher tax would encourage moonshining and bootlegging."

as now provided by law, except that the persons included in the proviso of this section shall not be considered subject to the provisions of this act until after the expiration of the license they may have applied for and obtained previous to the passage of this Act.

When another election may be held.

Sec. VI. *Be it further enacted by the authority aforsaid,* That if a majority of the votes cast at the election provided for in this Act shall be "Against prohibition" the ordinary of sais county may, upon recommendation of the grand jury and the petetion of one hundred citizens of said county order another election at which the same issue or question shall be submitted to the qualified voters of said county, that is "For prohihibition" and "Against pro-

Some rules to govern in new elections.

hibition." In the event another election shall be ordered for said purposesuch election shall be ordered and the notice given in the same manner as here inbefore provided. The returns of said election shall be made in the same manner and the result proclaimed in the same way as hereinbefore provided. In the event the majority of the votes cast at such second election shall be in favor of the prohibition, "For prohibition" of the sale of the aforesaid spirituous or intoxicating liquors or bitters , then all the provisions shall become and be of the same force and effect as if the majority of the votes cast at the first election held under this act had been in favor of prohibition "For prohibition" of the sale of intoxicating liquors

Second election-when ordered and how governed.

provided, a second election shall not be ordered sooner than twelve months after the first election; *provided further,* that in the event of majority of the votes cast at the first election under this Act are "For prohitition," then, and in that event, the ordinary shall, upon the recommendation of the grand jury, and the petetion of a hundred of the citizens of said county order a second election at which issue of "For prohibition" or "Against prohibition" of the sale or retail of spirituous or intoxicating liquors or bitters, shall be submitted to the qualified voters of said county, and all the subsequent proceedings shall be the same as hereinbefore provided for a second election, and if a majority of the votes cast at such second-election shall be "Against prohibition," then and in that event, the town and county authorities may issue license to retail spirituous or intoxicating liquors or bitters, under the rules and regulations prescribed by law.

Sec. VII. *Be it further enacted by the authority aforesaid,* That all laws and parts of laws in conflict with this Act be, and the same are hereby repealed.

Approved September 12, 1883.

Bill addressing prohibition in Georgia

In her writings, Smith continues by noting "while all this was happening, Granddaddy Lawrence and his two brothers, Warner, Jr. and Saunders Paul, were sent to live with a bachelor uncle, Paul, Jr., in Atlanta. Paul, Jr. and his father, Paul, Sr., were in the grocery store business together and it was with Paul, Jr. that Lawrence Lavalle Jones and his brothers grew up. Being a bachelor, Paul, Jr. lived in a hotel. He never took a house after the boys came to stay, so all three children lived in the hotel till they grew up."

The Jones' business thrived under the direction of Paul, Sr., until his death in 1877. Eighteen years later, Paul, Jr. died. An unknown writer for Paul, Jr.'s, obituary would say words to the effect

Paul Jones, Jr.

that a common remark about the two men was the close intimacy they both shared in life. They were hardly ever separated and went to and from meals together. It must have been a beautiful relationship for the two men who had already been through so much together.

Always the entrepreneur, Paul, Jr., expanded his business interests into whiskey sales and continued to run the business in such a way that he became a prominent citizen in the "New" Atlanta that quickly replaced the burned and battered shell left on the bones of the old one. His influence in city affairs was widely noticed and he became so strong in political circles that he could get city employees elected and appointed at will.

Well, the business took off and began to thrive and flourish under his leadership despite the best intentions of local prohibition activists who tried to put all alcohol beverage producers in Georgia out of business. Throughout the next few years, with his young nephews at his side, Paul, Jr. continued to run his business interests while leading the fight against the passage of any legislation that would lead to statewide prohibition.

In 1883, the opposition gained enough influence and power to succeed in passing legislation that brought about statewide prohibition in Georgia. With the lost legislative battles behind him and no doubt in his mind about the outcome, Paul, Jr. made the decision to look around for family business opportunities elsewhere.

CHAPTER TWO:

The Legend of Four Roses. 1883-1895

The Southern Exposition and the Move to Whiskey Row

It may very well have been the Southern Exposition of 1883 that attracted Paul, Jr.'s attention to Louisville, Kentucky.

This public relations move to showcase southern businesses was an attempt by a few businessmen to revive the north's interest in what the rebuilt business centers in the southern states had to offer as they struggled to get on their feet again.

Located in what is now the St. James Court district of Louisville, the exposition would have had displays of almost every conceivable type and description. Visitors came from far and near to marvel at many of the latest inventions available for viewing. It is not unlikely that Paul Jones, Jr. would have seen and been amazed by the impressive premier of Edison's electric light bulb. It was a display that lit up a city block and was surely hard to miss.

According to Lawrence L. Jones' oldest daughter, Louise, another reason may have influenced Paul, Jr.'s decision to select Louisville for a business location. It seems that he was on a trip to buy horses and visited a livery stable on Main Street owned by a Mr. Osborne. In addition to looking at the horses, he saw the whiskey trade offices close by and recognized the opportunities such a move might offer. He later sent for his nephews and other family members who were still in Atlanta. They took up lodging in the Galt House which was, at the time, located at the corner of Second and Main Streets.

The Galt House that they knew was the one completed in 1869 after fire destroyed the first one in 1865. It would be a favorite of U.S. presidents, from U.S. Grant to Theodore Roosevelt, as well as of noted entertainers, until it was torn down to make way for Belknap Hardware and Manufacturing Company's new headquarters and warehouse in 1919.

According to the late historian Ernest P. Ripy, years ago there was also a Galt House Hotel on Main Street in Lawrenceburg, Kentucky that was located close to the current Anderson County Court House.

For their new whiskey business offices, they first rented and then later purchased office space at 138 East Main Street. By the way, an old publication called *Caron's City Directory* first lists the Paul Jones business at 136-140 East Main in 1887. According to publications at the time, it doesn't seem to have taken very long for the business to have prospered from this location. Truly, the move to Louisville had been a smart one for the Jones family.

More than likely, the Joneses might have rubbed elbows and done business with other whiskey producers and rectifiers such as J.T.S. Brown, R.E. Wathen, W.L. Weller and I.W. Bernheim. This was the area in Louisville where all of the major whiskey producers maintained offices for their distilleries that were physically located around the city or in remote locations throughout the state of Kentucky.

The Main Street location also provided an easy access for the Joneses and the other whiskeymen to contract with Ohio River steamboat captains to transport their products through Shippingport on the northwest side of the city, then down through the western reaches of the Ohio to the Mississippi River at Cairo, Illinois. From there, they would be sent down-river to New Orleans, Louisiana, where they would be loaded on to either steam-powered packet boats or clipper ships, with their yards and yards of canvas sails, to be sold to customers along the east coast, in Europe or the Far East.

The Romance – A Brand is Born.

It was about this time, the early 1880s, that the legend of how the Four Roses name came about more than likely began.

Some say that it was Paul, Jr. that was smitten by a Southern Belle in the version of the story that ended up on the back label of our current 80 proof (40%) Four Roses Kentucky Straight Bourbon Whiskey. A few of the versions state that it happened in the Old South before the start of the Civil War. One version on the guide to the 1965 World's Fair in New York City even said that it happened in Lexington, Kentucky.

Katherine Jones Smith presented a different scenario when she wrote, "It was during this period that my grandfather (Lawrence Lavalle Jones) married my grandmother. Saunders was the first one to get married and his wife was a great friend of Mary Peabody's (her future grandmother.) Both girls were from Columbus (Georgia.) My grandfather met Mary Peabody when she would come up from her home in Columbus, Georgia, to visit Saunder's wife. He (her grandfather) was very shy and often he would rush away when she came into his presence. My grandmother was a very beautiful woman and at first would pay no attention to the shy, stern, homely man who sought her attentions. However, when my grandfather at last made up his mind to court her, he gave her no peace until the day he won her. He made frequent trips to Columbus to see Mary, each time asking her to marry him. This procedure went on for more than five years."

"Finally, when he was in Columbus for a large dance, he decided that he would ask her to marry him just once more and if the answer was no he would not ask her again."

She further wrote, "He sent my grandmother a dozen roses and in it he wrote this card – 'for over five years I have asked you to marry me. Tonight I ask you for the last time. If the answer is yes, wear a corsage of four roses, if it is no, don't wear any.'"

Having set the scene, she further related, "That night when she came down the steps dressed for the dance, I am sure Granddaddy's heart missed a few beats, for she wore a corsage of four roses. In his heart, he resolved to make that memory always last. Thus, to his best and most popular brand of whiskey he gave the name "Four Roses." Later versions of the legend would capitalize on this one but point the finger of origination at Paul Jones, Jr.

"1888"

It was about this time that Paul Jones, Jr. gets the credit for being the first person to register the trademark for the Four Roses name in the *Midas Criterion*. This publication listed businesses and their identifying marks in the days before it was necessary to register them with the federal government. It was a simple enough procedure to have it listed, and legal enough to maintain, that this trademark has remained unbroken through some of the most turbulent times in American history. Countless wars and economic upheavals have not damaged the validity of it, and it is as strong today as it was back then.

Family Tragedies

Sadness would strike the family with the untimely death of the oldest of the three nephews, Warner Paul Jones, Jr., in 1889. Considered to be the brightest and smartest of the three, he had been plagued by sickness through the years, had not played an active role in the family business and had never married.

Perhaps it was the death of Warner, Jr. that made Lawrence Lavalle express qualms to his family about working with his uncle in the whiskey business. But, according to information in the family's papers, a preacher encouraged him to continue in it rather than move to Baltimore, Maryland, where he would have preferred to live.

Up to this point, the Joneses had been in the business of rectifying the whiskey they were selling. That meant that they had bought a lot of whiskey from small distilleries then mixed and matched it to produce their brands. It was the way that a lot of companies got their start during the 1880s. Their attempt to buy, then run, the old Mattingly Distillery property in South Louisville was less than successful and ended when a portion of it burned.

Paul, Jr. Relents

Well, the idea of marriage between Lawrence Lavalle and Mary did not sit well with his uncle Paul. You see, it was his uncle's line of reasoning that marriage would interfere with Lawrence Lavalle's work as a top-ranking salesman for their company. A heated discussion followed, with Lawrence Lavalle threatening to quit and form his own company if his uncle did not give his blessing to the prospective marriage. Since Paul, Jr. adored both Lawrence Lavalle and Saunders Paul, he relented and raised both of his nephews to equal partnership with him in the company. When this was completed, Lawrence Lavalle and Mary Emma were married in 1894.

Mary Emma and Lawrence Lavalle Jones. Is the legend actually their story?

The Louisville Driving and Fair Association

Well, as you may recall, one of the reasons Paul Jones, Jr. came to Louisville in the first place was to buy some horses. This fascination with them, and trotting horses in particular, spread to his nephews as well. They were often seen driving a buggy and "giving way to no one" in the city streets, pulled by some of the finest trotting horses in Louisville.

In his book, *Churchill Downs – A Documentary History of America's Most Legendary Race Track*, author Dr. Samuel W. Thomas gives us an example of Paul, Jr.'s involvement with local trotting horse events, as evidenced in this quote from the book that came from *The Louisville Commercial Newspaper*, 22 October 1894.

Lawrence L. Jones, Jr.   *Saunders Paul Jones*

"The trotting horse organization known as the Louisville Driving and Fair Association was permanently formed on 6 August 1894 at the Galt House, with Paul Jones elected president and J.J. Douglas and John E. Green, vice presidents. Concern was voiced about the availability of Churchill Downs for a fall meet, and the following year a trotting track was constructed southeast of Churchill Downs…"

This fascination with horse racing was to be a family trait that would become prominent several decades later in the person of Warner L. Jones. A descendant of Saunders Paul Jones, with bloodlines connected to the Clarks and the Churchills, he was the grandson of the Clark that went west with Meriwether Lewis and also the grandson of a Churchill associated with a local race track that became the great Churchill Downs. He would later sit on the Board of Directors for Churchill Downs, before becoming chairman from 1984 to 1992.

He became the first person to breed and sell winners of the Kentucky Derby (Dark Star in 1953), Kentucky Oaks (Nancy Jr. in 1967) and Breeders' Cup Juvenile (Is It True in 1988). His horse business interests were headquartered at his Hermitage Farm located northeast of Louisville, near Goshen, Kentucky.

Paul Jones, Jr. 1895

Obituary of Paul Jones, Jr.

It happened so quickly that very few of Paul, Jr.'s friends knew that he was seriously ill, and his death was a great surprise to everyone.

He had gone about his business with his nephews as usual on a Friday morning. Later that afternoon, he complained about severe pains in his head and went home to his apartment in the Galt House. A short time later, he was taken to the Norton Infirmary.

The next morning, he seemed much better, but by 1:00 pm, his health began to worsen and he lapsed into unconsciousness. Newspaper accounts say that he stayed that way until a few moments before he passed away at age 55.

Bright's Disease, an inflammation and swelling of the kidneys was listed as the cause of death. The disease was in an advanced state when discovered a few days earlier by a doctor. The same doctor was heard to say it was the reason for death only a few short days later.

Paul Jones, Jr. Dies at 55

Paul Jones, Jr. died Friday of Bright's Diease. He had been largely instrumental in building up one of the largest whiskey trades in the south; and the business flourished extensively in his hands. Paul was a very rich man for these parts when prohibition broke up his business. His ability, however, was not confined to any particular place, and he succeeded as well in Louisvil' he did

This was an untreatable malady near the end of the 1800s and claimed a lot of lives. Most notable among them were President of the United States Chester A. Arthur and Alice Roosevelt, the wife of future American President Theodore ("Teddy") Roosevelt.

President Chester A. Authur

There was some early talk of bringing the body back to Atlanta for burial near his late brother Warner. But, in the end, he was finally laid to rest in the Jones family burial plot, located in Louisville's Cave Hill Cemetery, that can still be visited today.

Newspaper obituaries from Atlanta at the time said that he had "...been largely instrumental in building up one of the largest whiskey trades in the south; and the business flourished extensively in his hands." One further states that "Paul Jones was a very rich man for these parts when prohibition broke up his business. His ability, however, was not confined to any particular place, and he succeeded as well in Louisville as he did in Atlanta."

Alice Roosevelt

Such accolades and tributes were not surprising for a man of his stature. After all, he had been one of the first to believe in outdoor advertising and had, according to historian Mike Veach, "...rented space on a building in Madison Square (New York City) for a sign of incandescent electric lights at a cost of twelve hundred dollars a month." He could do this with the assurance that his name and that of his brands were becoming better known all across the United States.

Another commentary on his passing said that "Mr. Jones was quite a rich man at the time of his death. He was a thorough-going business man and the great fortune which he will leave is a fitting commentary upon his abilities as a merchant and financier." It goes further by stating that "two of his nephews, Lawrence and Saunders Jones, have been since childhood with Mr. Paul Jones and were associated with him in business at the time of his death." It then goes on to speculate that "In all probability they will succeed him in the firm which he established." And, did they ever.

Cave Hill Cemetary

President William Howard Taft put an end to the question of "What is Whiskey?"

CHAPTER THREE:

From Making Whiskey to Making Medicine. 1895-1934

The Paul Jones Company

Lawrence and Saunders continued to grow their late uncle's business despite the excesses of the "Golden Age" the United States experienced at the close of the 1900s. The turn of the century promised to bring nothing but better times for the Joneses and their business. They purchased their whiskies from distilleries in Louisville, Frankfort and Lawrenceburg, Kentucky. It was their plan to use the best in quality that they could find.

As mentioned earlier, the Paul Jones Company was listed in a copy of *Caron's City Directory* as 136 – 140 on East Main Street from 1887 until 1908. There must have been a consolidation of office space, and it appears that a notation in 1909 lists a new address as between 118 and 122 East Main Street, with other professional businesses listed at the same address.

Main Street, Louisville, 1900

Well, as the successful are often want to do, the nephews decided that they needed a building to call their own. For that reason, they financed the construction of the Paul Jones Building in Louisville at the corner of Fourth and Liberty Streets and moved into it in 1907.

The Taft Decision

While the Jones name and the Four Roses brand were not listed as the center of the public controversy about the answer to the question of "What is Whiskey," they were terribly interested in what was taking place on a national level.

On June 30, 1906, the government put into place the Pure Food and Drug Act. With shaky clarity about what would be "pure" whiskey. The government had to first decide what whiskey was all about.

There were two schools of thought about it. The first stated that whiskey was only a distilled spirit from fermented grain mash that was then aged in charred oak barrels using only pure water to adjust the final proof before consumption. On the other side, the second idea was that the term "whiskey" referred to a distilled spirit that was altered by combining it with neutral grain alcohol, burnt sugar or caramel and either artificial or natural coloring agents.

As luck would have it, the chief chemist for the Department of Agriculture under Theodore Roosevelt decided that the first version was true and not the second one. This had a highly unfavorable response from that part of the whiskey industry that the Joneses were in called "rectifiers" – the folks that purchased bulk whiskey, then blended it with neutral grain alcohol and added other things to make a flavor profile their dedicated customers could identify. This ruling also upset the import market and interestingly led to the term "imitation whiskey" being applied to such venerable products as Canadian, Scotch and Irish whiskies.

All of this caused the Paul Jones Company to scramble fast to assure their followers that everything they said about their whiskies was true. In Harvard Square in New York City at the intersection of Broadway, Sixth Avenue and 34th Street, Paul Jones & Co. proclaimed on placards that "WE GUARANTEE OUR WHISKIES TO CONFORM TO THE UNITED STATES PURE FOOD LAWS."

WHISKY PLEA TO TAFT.

Decision in Dispute Under Pure Food Law Now Left to President.

WASHINGTON, June 19.—President Taft received to-day from John G. Carlisle and Edmund W. Taylor, representing the "stright" whisky interests in the recent controvery as to what is whisky, their statement of exceptions to the findings of Solicitor General Bowers. Both sides having now taken exceptions to Mr. Bowers's ruling, the President, as final arbiter in the case, will probably fix a time for a hearing on the subject.

The controversy turns upon the point as to whether or not whisky, which has been aged by higher rectification, is entitled to rank as whisky along with that aged in charred oak barrels, or whether under the pure food law it should be labeled an imitation or compound whisky because of the introduction of neutral spirits during the process of rectification.

The New York Times
Published: June 20, 1909
Copyright © The New York Times

Others joined in this war of words with the straight whiskey distillers labeling their products as "Pure Food" under the law, while the rectifiers were still able to call their products "Whiskey."

The year 1909 saw Roosevelt out and William Howard Taft in as president of the United States. It was Taft, from a very influential Ohio family, who waded into the fray and made it his business to put an end to the question of "What is Whiskey" and how the act was to be enforced.

Both sides argued for almost half a year as Taft listened and pondered over the definition. In the end, it all boiled down to a decision that nobody really liked. Simply stated, it said that the neutral spirits used in "Blended Whiskey" had to be made from grain instead of other things that could be identified with different alcoholic beverages. For example, since molasses was the basic ingredient of rum, it could not be used to make whiskey. The decision goes further by defining what could be called "straight whiskey," "blended whiskey" or even "imitation whiskey," as Taft thought it should be called.

Historian Mike Veach captured the spirit of this decision in an article he prepared about "The Taft Decision: One Century Later" in the Winter, 2009 edition of *The Bourbon Review.* He wrote: "One hundred years later when a person reads the regulations for a straight Bourbon or rye, they are reading the Taft Decision. There have been some additions to the decision over the years. Bourbon has to be aged in new barrels (1938) and is a product of the United States (1964), but the core regulations are the same as Taft laid down in 1909 with his decision as to 'What is Whiskey?'"

The Small-Grain Distilling Company

It was during this time that Lawrence Lavalle Jones and others formed the "Small-Grain Distilling Company" in an attempt to sell Four Roses straight whiskey through the mail. This business model, both witty and clever, catered to a small select list of customers. It was still in place as a company until national Prohibition was repealed in 1933.

This postcard attempted to sell whiskey through the mail.

The Family Explosion!

There was thought to be a separation between Saunders Paul and Lawrence Lavalle Jones over the business. Here is a condensed version of the families' writings about it.

In every family where there are two strong wills such as Lawrence and Saunders, there is bound to be controversy. Saunders had left the business for some reason known only to the family before national Prohibition was a reality.

Lawrence Lavalle had bought up his brother's shares at a fair price and the whiskey business was his. The rest is history.

Whether Saunders wanted to buy back into the business later at the price the shares were previously worth or whether it was because of some personal differences, the cause of argument between the two brothers remains unknown. However, the separation was a bitter one and their families did not speak to each other until after Saunders died. In the interim, Saunders and his family moved to New York state to live.

Saunders Paul Jones, 1916

Saunders Paul Jones died in 1916. A tribute to him said "He was a senior member of the Paul Jones Distilling Company and had interests in the Louisville Soap Company, Quaker Maid Stores, Jenkins Lubricator and the Paul Jones Building.

The tribute goes on to say that he was married to a certain La Boudie Barnett of Columbus, Georgia and that their children included: Paul Jones, Warner L. Jones, Mrs. John Churchill (one and the same), Saunders P. Jones, Jr., and Barnett Jones.

Saunders Paul Jones

Lead Up to National Prohibition

Some say that the forces that advocated national Prohibition had been around ever since the first colonists came ashore at both Jamestown and Plymouth in the 1600s. It was a constant battle that had outlived countless political upheavals, economic disasters and national emergencies.

With the advent of the three tier "system," the bar, gambling and prostitution, the American population was fueled for a change. This "system" simply meant that in most street corner saloons, the drinking was done on the first floor, gambling on the second and in some cases prostitution was ramped on the third.

To top it off, with a bar on virtually every corner in the manufacturing and business districts of the United States, fewer and fewer paychecks were making it intact into the American home in the early years of the twentieth century.

You might find it of interest to know that at the start of World War I, the tax on whiskey stood at $1.10 a gallon; at the end of that war it was $6.40.

When the Country was Wet and the Law was Dry

In *The Book of Frankfort* that was published in 1946 : "For the exclusive use of Frankfort Personnel and Wholesalers of Frankfort Products," there is this synopsis of what made the forces for national Prohibition unite and make it happen on January 16, 1919.

In the writer's opinion, it goes without saying that liquor was abused. Those who abuse it have always been in the minority. (A little perspective: two Yale University scientists, who have studied the problem recently, state that, of the 40,000,000 users of alcoholic beverages in the United States today, only five or six percent abuse it.)

But minorities are often more conspicuous than majorities. And the abuse of liquor by a minority was sufficiently conspicuous to give rise to temperance societies which, in turn, led to the Prohibition movement.

Pouring out whiskey from barrels during Prohibition

Historically, the written accounts from that era noted that in 1851, the state of Maine voted to go dry and this started a Prohibition wave across the country. In theory, it was thought that as Maine went, so eventually would the nation. But though the movement made great headway in the rural districts of the country, national Prohibition was scoffed at until World War I. Then the Prohibitionists, taking advantage of the mood of patriotic fervor to conserve food and manpower, as well as leveraging the fact that millions of male voters were fighting "over there," pushed their amendment through. When the nation finally got around to waking up, it found itself saddled with national Prohibition.

Amendments to the Constitution of the United States
Amendment 18 (1919)

1. After one year from the ratification of this article the manufacture, sale, or transportation of intoxicating liquors within, the importation thereof into, or the exportation thereof from the United States and all territory subject to the jurisdiction therof for beverage purposes is hereby prohibited.

2. The Congress and the several States shall have concurrent power to enforce this article by appropriate legislation.

3. This article shall be inoperative unless it shall have been ratified as an amendment to the Constitution by the legislatures of the several states, as provided in the Constitution, within seven years from the date of the submission hereof to the States by the Congress.

When it was made public that distilleries could apply for licenses in the early 1920s to sell whiskey for "Medicinal Purposes Only," Lawrence Lavalle's Frankfort Distilling Corporation, ably assisted by Messrs. S.C. Miller, William H. Veeneman and a host of others, opportunistically obtained a license for this purpose. Only six companies, the Schenley Distillers Corporation, the American Medicinal Spirits Company (later the National Distillers Products Co.), James Thompson and Brother (later called Glenmore Distillers Co.), the Brown-Forman Distillery Company, and the A. Ph. Stitzel Distillery, along with Frankfort Distilleries, Inc., were licensed by the government to supply one-hundred-proof bonded spirits for this purpose.

The sale of these "medicinal" products relied on previously produced whiskeys before 1919, since most of the distilleries were required to shut down and then sell off any distillation equipment to scrap dealers. These dealers were realistic enough to realize that the "noble experiment" would in time fail and for that reason held on to most of the equipment, which in turn would later be sold back to many of its original owners.

The way medicinal whiskey worked was like this: pads of prescriptions were obtained by doctors who would then, for a fee, issue them to patients in need.

"Patients" could obtain whiskey during Prohibition with a medical prescription.

These "patients" would then take their prescriptions to druggists who would, for a fee, fill them with whiskey obtained from consolidation warehouses where most producers were forced to sell their aged whiskies in order to obtain what little money they could during this dark period in beverage alcohol history.

It may be of interest to note that this "Medicinal Purposes Only" practice was so widespread that a shortage of reliable legal whiskey soon existed in the United States. To compensate for this shortage, a distiller's "Holiday" was declared in 1928 to replenish the stocks of Medicinal Whiskey. The distilleries that had the licenses to vend were allowed to produce a combined total of 3.2 million gallons to fill this need. Since most had either dismantled their distillery equipment or did not own distilleries at the time, A. Ph. Stitzel made the entire amount for all of them and any records of the percentage of how much each one could order has been lost over time.

A number of innovative forms of packaging for retail sales had been a Four Roses' hallmark, even before 1920. For example, a patent had been granted to the company for a bottle with a pouring device that made it impractical to refill. This was necessary to reduce the chances that someone could tamper with, or alter, the contents in such a way as to be detrimental to sales of the brand while under Paul Jones Co. ownership. The construction of the closure was such that the one-way valve could get stuck in the closed position. For that reason, there were instructions in each container that said: "NOTICE! Should bottle refuse to pour, apply lip suction at opening to release lower valve."

After combining with the Frankfort Distillery, a fiberboard box with a tamper-proof seal was patented to ensure that the contents were as advertised when it left the bottling facility. Government inspectors checking shipments sent to druggists recognized the containers and allowed them to go through for this reason.

Another reference in *The Book of Frankfort* notes that: "Prohibition taught America that you cannot vote liquor out of existence – you can only vote away its legality." It further states that "…in those unforgettable days from 1920 to 1933, the country learned what it means to have illegal liquor. Gangsters replaced distillers; bootleggers and speakeasy operators replaced respected salesmen and tavern-keepers. Instead of the smooth, palatable products of modern distilleries, we had rotgut, moonshine and bathtub gin. The government lost one of its chief sources of revenue, and thousands of men lost their jobs. Gang rule succeeded legal government in many cities, and deaths from poisonous liquor mounted."

At this point, the book's writers editorialized when it came to "Repeal." They wrapped their thoughts around the fact that "The fight against Prohibition started almost as soon as Prohibition became law. But the dies were firmly cast; it was a slow, uphill fight. Not until Franklin D. Roosevelt, an avowed and vocal champion of Repeal, was elected president did the cloud of Prohibition pass from the sky."

Fortunately, Lawrence Lavalle's insistence on maintaining the high quality of the brand soon made "Four Roses" a household name lasting through Prohibition, Repeal, and The Great Depression and all through the 1930s. Extensive advertising in magazines and periodicals also helped to promote the brand and to reinforce its colorful history after Repeal.

We have a bottle and its original cardboard container on display in the Four Roses Visitor's Center at the distillery that is from this time period. It has a closure that says, "SEAL PREVENTS TAMPERING AND INSURES PURITY." Other labeling indicates, "Four Roses Spiritus Frumenti 100 PROOF AN ALCOHOLIC STIMULANT MADE FROM THE FERMENTED MASH OF GRAIN" "AGED IN WOOD." The Bottled in Bond Strip Stamp indicates that it was prepared at the "G.G. WHITE Co. Distillery No. 9, Kentucky" and "BOTTLED AT DISTILLERY BONDED WAREHOUSE NO. 33 DISTRICT OF KY" "BOTTLED FALL 1923 MADE SPRING 1914". The SPARKS DRUG STORE label, from SPARKS, NEVADA, attached over the back label indicating that it was "Bottled at The Frankfort Distillery" and among other things lists under "Directions: 2 ounces in hot water" and the "Date Filled Sept 16 - 24". It was packaged inside a paperboard container that is different from later ones of the same era.

The Frankfort Distillery

In a more productive venture, the Paul Jones Company, under the leadership of Jones and Veeneman, scrambled to acquire the Frankfort Distilling Company and combined the two in order to form the Frankfort Distilling Corporation in 1922.

Known previously as the W. J. Baker Brothers & Co. Distillery before 1903, it would bear a number of names including "Swastika" before it became the Frankfort Distillery, 1905-1916. It was located four miles east of Frankfort, Kentucky, on the Georgetown Pike, one mile west of the junction of the North and South Elkhorn Creek on the Frankfort and Cincinnati Railroad line. This railroad, designed to connect with major rail lines leading to Louisville and Cincinnati, would have been the "Bourbon Express" of its time.

During the period of 1923 to 1933, the Frankfort Distillery also had the misfortune to encounter three large fires. Here was whiskey burning up and no more being made. At the end of Prohibition, whiskey again came into its own and the company now adopted the name of Frankfort Distilleries, Incorporated.

The Eagle Roller Mill

The Parting of the Clouds

The year 1933 ushered in the Roosevelt era resplendent with the "New Deal" concept for the United States, and with it came the repeal of the 18th Amendment, on December 5, 1933, that was so desperately needed to kick-start the government's loss of taxation revenue due to Prohibition. If you have never read it, here is what the 21st Amendment looks like.

Amendments to the Constitution of the United States
Amendment 21 (1933)

1. The eighteenth article of amendment to the Constitution of the United States is hereby repealed.

2. The transportation or importation into any State, Territory, or possession of the United States for delivery or use therein of intoxicating liquors, in violation of the laws thereof, is hereby prohibited.

3. The article shall be inoperative unless it shall have been ratified as an amendment to the Constitution by conventions in the several States, as provided in the Constitution, within seven years from the date of the submission hereof to the States by the Congress.

New Facilities

With the need to obtain a license to sell medicinal whiskey during national Prohibition, the Paul Jones Company purchased the Frankfort Distillery Company and underwent company reorganization. They then bought the Stitzel Distillery on Story Avenue in Louisville's "Butchertown." After operating at this location for a few years, they built a new distillery south of Louisville in Shively. This plant was also known as The Four Roses Distillery because of its principal brand. The old Story Avenue location was closed after a number of years. In 1943, the Frankfort Distillery was sold to Seagram, which operated it until 1972.

Never mentioned again.

Katherine Jones Smith, granddaughter of Lawrence Lavalle, would mention in her writings that, "In 1933, Grandmother (Mary Peabody Jones) died. She came down with pneumonia, and three days later she was dead. This caused great sorrow to my grandfather and for some unknown reason her name was never mentioned again in his presence." (It is said that his grief was so severe, he had her room sealed and her car wrapped in brown paper so no one could drive it.) "All the grandchildren quickly learned that they were never to mention grandmother's name in front of him."

CHAPTER FOUR:

Back to the drawing board! 1934 -1943

Times Square in New York

As a side note, during the latter part of the 19th century, outdoor advertising decorated everything from wagons to buildings. Paul Jones had rented space in New York City's Madison Square for what was then only available for public view in daylight, since the availability and high cost of street lights held little excitement for the general public.

Cheaper light bulbs and a wiring system that was soon envied by Philadelphia were mounted on tall poles and increased the number of people who suddenly felt free, and safer, to walk the streets at night to go to the theater, have dinner in the many restaurants in the area and, of course, read the advertisements posted on building walls.

As the city grew and expanded away from the docks of Manhattan, the fashionable district moved from Madison Square to Herald Square. Named for the *International Herald Tribune* – which was founded in 1887 and headquartered at the intersection of Broadway, Sixth Avenue, and 34th Street – Herald Square was the home of two of the largest retail stores in the world, Gimbel's and Macy's.

"Spectacular"

Five years after the repeal of Prohibition, advertising for Four Roses would reach a high point, with lighted outdoor advertising in New York City's Times Square. The original design concept was the product of a long forgotten advertising firm. Employed by Frankfort, the firm was to come up with a startling concept to further the brand's acceptance by a public that was once more prepared to enjoy Four Roses Bourbon after a long absence from retail shelves. No longer would customers have to be humbled to pay for a doctor's office visit to obtain a prescription to take to a druggist where, for more money, they could receive a small portion of their "medicine."

The outdoor design called for a spiral of roses on either side of the name "Four Roses" at the top. These spirals would "grow" from the bottom to the top on both sides on a time-released mechanism that would electrically illuminate the green vines and leaves as well as the red roses that were all done in both neon and standard light bulbs. The center of the main panel would then go dark and be followed by a second exhibit that read, "A Truly Great Whiskey!" It was a "Times Square Spectacular" according to Darby Tell in her book of the same name. The big sign premiered in 1938 and remained in operation through the end of 1945.

With the advent of the Second World War in 1941, the United States was put on full war-time security alert. This was to have an adverse but prideful impact on the Four Roses sign in Times Square during World War II. In short, with close encounters to back it up, and since it was

Left: The name Four Roses sits atop the other famous American brand names in Times Square, from 1938 – 1945.

Famous photo by Alfred Eisenstaedt taken in Times Square at the end of World War II. Notice the sign at the top in the background.

indeed visible from as far away as the Statue of Liberty in New York Harbor, it was turned off at dark in order to reduce the possibility of it being used as a target by German submarines that were known to be prowling off the New Jersey coast.

By the way, there is a copy of the famous Alfred Eisenstaedt photograph of a sailor kissing a nurse in Times Square in celebration of the absolute end of World War II that shows this sign in the background. The sign isn't often seen when the cropped version is reproduced.

Irwin S. Cobb

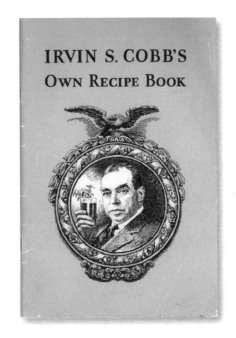

Irwin S. Cobb, a popular newspaper columnist, humorist and actor of that time was commissioned by Frankfort Distillers to author a book entitled, *Irvin S. Cobb's Own Recipe Book.* This fancifully written work, according to Cobb, contained "authoritative directions for making 71 famous drinks, together with a rollicking dissertation of the joys of King Bourbon and its Brother Rye, by the famous Kentuckian." It was offered by mail-order for 10 cents a copy. According to the book's foreword, Cobb was "born and bred in ol' Kaintucky, where prime Bourbon ranks with beautiful women and fast horses as the favored toast of the citizenry. He has personally experimented with the delights of whiskey in all its manifestations. And in his novel, *Red Likker,* he brought to American literature the best story of whiskey-making ever written."

Under the heading of "AMERICA'S LARGEST INDEPENDENT DISTILLING ORGANIZATION," Cobb took dramatic license with the Jones family story and mixed fact with fancy to the point that perhaps Paul Jones, Jr. had been a lieutenant in a Virginia Regiment. He writes that the lieutenant "turned homeward from the Civil War battlefield to find his house in ruins and his family destitute." Sadly, there is no record showing Paul Jones, Jr. or his rank in the Confederate Army in family history.

In 1935, the famous ad, "MOONLIGHT AND FOUR ROSES," appeared, extolling the "Four Roses Legend." In part, the copy reads, "In the glamorous days before the War between the States, a young gentleman named Paul Jones laid siege to the heart and hand of a lovely Southern Belle.

With the charming coquetry of that gallant age, she signified her acceptance of his suit by wearing to a cotillion a corsage of four red roses.

It is from this incident in a gracious past that Four Roses – a blend of straight whiskies – drew its name. And we are proud to invite you to make it a part of your own gracious scheme of living. You'll find it superb liquor – fragrant as Southern flowers, mellow as the moonlight shining on them."

There is no positive proof to connect Cobb directly to this concept but it does resemble his purloined prose in both the cookbook and *Red Likker.* The fascination with the Southern Belle concept continues to this day as a source of the mystique and romance of the Four Roses story.

MOONLIGHT AND FOUR ROSES

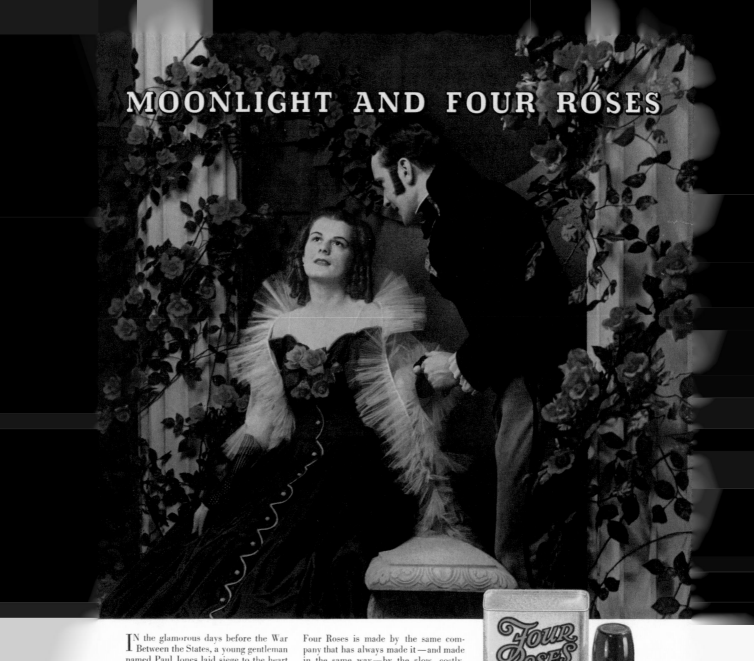

IN the glamorous days before the War Between the States, a young gentleman named Paul Jones laid siege to the heart and hand of a lovely Southern belle.

With the charming coquetry of that gallant age, she signified her acceptance of his suit by wearing to a cotillion a corsage of *four red roses*.

It is from this incident in a gracious past that Four Roses—a blend of straight whiskies—drew its name. And we are proud to invite you to make it a part of your own gracious scheme of living. You'll find it a superb liquor—fragrant as Southern flowers, mellow as the moonlight shining on them.

Four Roses is made by the same company that has always made it—and made in the same way—by the slow, costly, old-fashioned method.

Four Roses Whiskey is reasonably priced. Try a bottle. *Insist* on it at hotels and restaurants.

Send 10¢ for "IRVIN S. COBB'S OWN RECIPE BOOK."

Other Frankfort Whiskies: PAUL JONES—*a blend of straight whiskies* • OLD OSCAR PEPPER—*a blend of straight whiskies* • SHIPPING PORT—*straight whiskey* • ANTIQUE—*whiskey, a blend* • MATTINGLY & MOORE—*whiskey, a blend.*

 Lovers of fine gin will appreciate the rare flavor of Paul Jones ★★★★ Gin

FOUR ROSES WHISKEY

A blend of all straight whiskies

Made by Frankfort Distilleries of Louisville, Ky., and Baltimore, Md.

America's largest independent distillers

The Great Depression

The Great Depression afforded another opportunity for creative label design. One story alluded to the idea that the direction of the roses on the label had been changed from hanging downward to a more upward position and that the type of rose was changed to a variety know as "Better Times" in order to give a sense of hope to consumers in those uncertain times.

Label with roses facing downward

New, more hopeful, label with roses pointing up

Egg Nog: 1936

With the banner headline of ONCE AGAIN…IT'S TIME TO MAKE A BOWL OF MERRY CHRISTMAS! Frankfort Distilleries launched a holiday campaign that would become a favorite with consumers for many years to come.

It had an elegant silver punch bowl, cups and sprigs of holly thrown in for good measure. The ad copy says in part that "If we didn't know the month or day – if we couldn't find a calendar high or low – we'd still be kept right up to date by the annual flood of requests we get at this time for our Four Roses Egg nog recipe."

Well, guess what? It is still the same with emails today. We are still getting requests for reprints of the recipe.

Some modern day writers reveal personal glimpses of family history when they tell us that they can still remember when their mother cut the recipe out of a magazine, made it, then reverently folded it and carefully placed it in the family's cookbook in order to use it from year-to-year.

Lawrence Lavalle Jones

The year 1941 witnessed the end of the Jones family's involvement with the Four Roses brand and Frankfort Distilleries when Paul Jones' last nephew, Lawrence Lavalle Jones, died. The last principal owner of the Frankfort Distilleries Incorporated died of pneumonia on October 21, 1941.

His wife, the former Mary Peabody, of Columbus, Georgia, and a son, Lawrence L. Jones, Jr., had died several years earlier. He was survived by three daughters, Mrs. Baylor O. Hickman, Mrs. Henry Fitzhugh, Jr., and Mrs. Frazier Lebus, and eleven grandchildren.

In addition to the whiskey business, Mr. Jones was connected with and was principal owner of the Jefferson Island Salt Company and the Peerless Manufacturing Company.

He was also known to participate in many civic activities. In fact, he was one of the prime motivators in making the Kentucky State Fair a permanent institution in Louisville.

Lawrence Lavalle Jones

The obituary further states that he was known as an avid horseman and maintained stables of the finest saddle and show horses in the world. It also says that he sent entries to Kentucky county fairs as well as to big shows throughout the nation. His horse, Poetry In Motion, was several times winner of the three gaited saddle horse class of the International Horse Show in Chicago. The horse was never beaten in any competitive event across the country.

Kentucky State Fairgrounds

He was a director of the American Turf Association that controlled Churchill Downs as well as other race tracks in Latonia, Kentucky and Chicago, Illinois.

Upon his death, the Jones family pondered the fate of the company that was now in the throes of a major global war effort. With the loss of major foreign suppliers of rubber to the enemy during those critical early days of the war, the government turned to the distilleries to make synthetic rubber, as well as to produce munitions components and medical supplies. It proved to be a mandate that required high-proof alcohol manufacturing on a grand scale. Beverage alcohol production was curtailed, which led to increased values placed on aging whiskey in warehouses throughout the country. Every available distilling company was given the task of increasing their production to the point that even small rural distilleries were contracted to make spirits that could then be turned into war-time materials.

By 1941, the tax on whiskey was $4 a gallon. It soon went to $6 in 1942.

"I'll light Louisville."

In addition to the whiskey business, Mr. Jones was connected with and principal owner of the Jefferson Island Salt Company, the Peerless Manufacturing Company, coal mining, chain stores and the Kentucky Electric Company.

The Kentucky Electric Company came about as a result of an architectural mistake concerning the top three floors of the Paul Jones Building at 4th and Liberty in Louisville. Plans for electrical service to them had been overlooked in the estimates for the building, resulting in Jones being charged a higher rate than a couple of nearby stores. When he complained to the electric provider for a lower rate, he was told, "If you want a (lower) rate, make your own light." He reportedly stormed out of their offices and said "I'll light Louisville." He quickly formed a corporation known as the Kentucky Electric Company in order to get a cheaper rate for both himself and the people of Louisville. It proved so successful that is was finally taken over by the Louisville Gas and Electric Company.

In 1943, Seagram president and owner, Samuel Bronfman, purchased the Four Roses brand for $42 million.

CHAPTER FIVE:

Seagram Buys the Brand. 1943 -1971

Sam Bronfman and Seagram

Whiskey already aging in barrels before the war started was a precious commodity. As a result, Canadian Samuel Bronfman, owner of Joseph E. Seagram & Sons, Inc., soon became interested in acquiring not only a number of whiskies but also their nationally known trademarks to further their alcoholic beverage interests. It was Mr. Sam's intention to stretch out these stored goods by using them in his highly popular blended whiskies, since he believed that the war would drag on for more years than it actually did.

In 1943, he proposed an offer for all of Frankfort Distilleries in both Kentucky and Maryland, its trademarks and stores of aging whiskies. According to Nicolas Faith in his book, *The Bronfmans – The Rise and Fall of the House of Seagram*, "Sam's most important wartime investment came in 1943 with the purchase (for a seemingly expensive $42 million) of a famous business, Frankfort Distilleries in Louisville, the country's fifth largest liquor business, which included two major brands, Four Roses and Paul Jones. He bought it from family shareholders who had recently inherited the business and were anxious to avoid paying taxes by selling it. In a move that showed his obsession with blended whiskey, Sam converted Four Roses from a straight whiskey to a blend in the 1950s. (It is interesting to note that Four Roses had been sold for export as a straight Bourbon whiskey when owned by Frankfort, and that it continued to be exported as such to Europe and Japan under the new ownership.) More relevantly, so far as Mr. Sam was concerned, Frankfort had one of the most important stocks of aging Bourbon in the whole country – twenty million gallons. Mr. Sam's credit rating was good enough to enable him to raise $75 million – well above the $42 million he needed to buy Frankfort – from two major banks, in the form of a revolving credit line. Such finance was crucial in what *Fortune* magazine described as a "banking and inventory business," with the need to store whiskey for four or more years and then pay a tax of $9 a gallon to the federal government when it was taken out of bond to be blended and sold.

As a result, by 1946 Mr. Sam was able to control the whole production chain from raw material to the bottle in the liquor store. The whiskies, grain and straight, came from fourteen distilleries in Canada and the United States. The whiskies they produced were matured in sixty warehouses and bottled in ten bottling plants across North America. By 1948, Seagram owned three of the top ten brands: Seven Crown, Calvert Reserve, and Four Roses." In short, Four Roses had moved from the realm of a much-respected family business into the arena of a Fortune 500 company.

1944 – 11 Years After Repeal

In 1944, the whiskey tax soared to $9 a gallon. It stayed that way until after the war when it reverted to $6.

According to information from the The Book of Frankfort*: "In the fiscal year ending June 30, 1944, the alcoholic beverage industry contributed in federal, state and local taxes the sum of one billion, nine hundred million dollars.*

During the 11 years since repeal, the alcoholic beverage industry has contributed, in federal, state and local taxes, the gigantic sum of 13 billion dollars. So you see that, instead of spending billions to try to enforce an unenforceable law with all of its attendant crime, our government has drawn from a legitimate industry huge sums for the security, comfort and progress of all our people."

A Network of Distilleries

Part of the Seagram distilling complex was a network of five distilleries in Kentucky. With the exception of the Calvert Distillery on Seventh Street Road in Louisville, all of the individual facilities had been purchased in the mid-1940s to supply Bourbon for Seagram's famous blended whiskies that had gained so much acceptance during and after repeal. Each of these five distilleries is important to the development of the Four Roses Brand as it exists today, as each one of our five proprietary yeast strains currently in use originated at one of them.

Calvert on Seventh Street Road

Seagram's main center for corporate authority was located at the Calvert Distillery on Seventh Street Road, in Louisville, Kentucky. It was built in 1937 and operated as both the Calvert Distillery RD # 37 and the Julius Kessler Distilling Company.

In New York, management decided that with a decline in consumer preference for the distillery's whiskey production in the 1970s and the fact that other Seagram plants in Lawrenceburg, Indiana and Relay, Maryland, could more cheaply absorb the plant's bottling and finished goods distribution, it was time to phase it out. This resulted in the on-site barrel warehouse inventory being gradually depleted with any new production being sent to storage facilities in Jeffersonville, Indiana.

Due to 1978 state legislation that dramatically increased taxes on maturing inventories, the fate of the Kentucky operation was in question. It was only through a reversal in a state bill that things stayed status quo.

By 1982, even the future of the Cox's Creek facility was in doubt and the distillery in Lawrenceburg, Kentucky was slated to run only for six months every two years.

Finally, in 1983, all activities at the Seventh Street Road location ceased and the property was sold.

Education and the Arts

Early management at the Calvert Distillery encouraged employee enlightenment by arranging for educational seminars to be conducted periodically on the grounds during lunch time. Employees could also check out works of art from the main office building to hang in their homes similar to the way we, sans *computer, check out library books today.*

The Other Four Distilleries

The Old Lewis Hunter Distillery

The Old Lewis Hunter Distillery in Cynthiana was another Bronfman acquisition. Tracing its origins back to 1850, the distillery was operated under a number of owners until Julius Kessler bought it in 1902. Kessler then introduced the Old Lewis Hunter brand and was challenged by the makers of the well-known Hunter Rye brand in Baltimore, Maryland. Kessler claimed the name belonged to an early settler who made whiskey nearby. Despite the fact that no proof of such a person was ever produced, Kessler used the name anyway. Mr. Sam purchased the distillery for his distilling empire in the 1950s and operated it periodically until 1976. After that, the distillery buildings were converted into business spaces, one of which housed an industrial hard hat factory.

The Athertonville Distillery

The Athertonville Distillery had a heritage that stretched back to 1800. It is a fact that Thomas Lincoln, father of the future president and resident of nearby Knob Creek, worked there and that Abe assisted his father until the family moved to Illinois.

Despite economic ups and downs, the distillery survived and, according to one account, "owned the entire town…which included 75 houses, a general store, a 100-room hotel, blacksmith shops and livery stables. In addition to the three miles of railroad track the company also owned its own locomotive to handle its own rail cars for grain, coal and whiskey."

Seagram purchased it in 1946 and ran it periodically as a Bourbon-producing distillery. After a fire destroyed the facility in the late 1970s, it was rebuilt and automated in 1979. The quality of the distillate was questionable. The property was sold by Seagram in 1987.

Athertonville Distillery

Worker at the Henry McKenna Distillery

The Henry McKenna Distillery

One of the many distilleries in Nelson County, the Henry McKenna Distillery, was founded by an Irish immigrant in the 1850s. Upon his death in 1892, his three sons carried on the business. The distillery and the brand name (but not the proprietary yeast strain) were also bought by Seagram in the 1940s as part of its post-Prohibition American expansion program. The distillery ceased operation in 1969. In 1976, the Fairfield, Kentucky property was dismantled and sold to private parties.

The Old Prentice Distillery

The Old Prentice Distillery outside of Lawrenceburg, Kentucky, was built in 1910 with the first production coming out in 1911. It is across Bonds Mill Road from the still visible foundations of the old powerhouse for the JTS Brown Distillery that was raised to make room for the graceful mission-architectural-styled main building that Four Roses calls home today. The JTS Brown Distillery was on the grounds of the old Waterfill and Frazier Distillery that originated in the 1870s.

Workers at the Old Prentice Distillery

The location was ideal due to the fact that the Eagle Roller Mill, a nearby source for milled grain, was located across from the new distillery on the other side of a good limestone water source, the Salt River. The mill was powered by what was then termed "the largest over-shot water-wheel on the east side of the Mississippi River."

Running alcohol was an occupation that suited Anderson County very well. As the story goes, Old Joe Peyton, an early frontier farmer, came through the Cumberland Gap and into the Kentucky River area prior to 1818. He made his way first to Harrodsburg and then by canoe on the Kentucky River to the banks of Gilbert's Creek where, due to the purity of the water, he erected a still and went into the whiskey-making trade. The distillery's old stone foundation is still visible next to Gilbert's Creek Road as it gets closer to the Kentucky River.

Some say that Old Joe spawned the beginning of an industry that prospered and grew, making the "Old Joe" brand one of the first advertised brands of whiskey at the turn of the century in 1800. It survived several ownerships until it finally went out of business at the beginning of national Prohibition in 1919.

George Prentice

The new distillery was named Old Prentice in honor of a fiery newspaper editor in Louisville named George Prentice, who was greatly admired by the Brown family who had it built.

Since the Old Prentice Distillery did not run from 1920 until 1933, the venerable name and reputation of "Old Joe" was resurrected by a widow named Agnes Brown (wife of the deceased Col. Davis Brown) and a well-known Anderson County distiller named Gratz B. Hawkins.

Moo!

It may be of interest to note that there are remains of a cattle feeding operation behind the distillery that were used until the Drier House was built in the 1960s. At its height, several thousand head of cattle were part of the operation to use up everything that wasn't turned to alcohol. It was permanently closed for environmental issues in 1970.

The distillery ran as Old Joe until 1942 and then was owned by Schenley, National Distillers, Grosscurths, and Julius Kessler before it was purchased by Seagram in 1946. Under Seagram, it did business as a number of distilling companies. It ended up as Old Prentice until that name and the Eagle Rare brand were both sold to Sazarac in 1988. In 1994, it became the Four Roses Distillery. It remained the Four Roses Distillery even after Kirin purchased it in 2002 from Diageo who had bought it from Vivendi when Seagram went out of business in 2000. Over time, this distillery has provided the Bourbon for "Old Baker," "Old Prentice," "Benchmark," "Eagle Rare" and Four Roses Export.

An early view of the Old Joe Distillery, later called the Old Prentice Distillery. Today, the Four Roses Distillery occupies the same building.

Five Down to One

Starting in the 1960s, as the American drinking public's preference for alcoholic beverages switched from brown goods to vodkas and wines, one by one, these small distilleries and the brands they supported were sold to competitors or phased out all together. With the closing of the Louisville plant, the Old Prentice Distillery, known today as Four Roses, and Cox's Creek along with Corporate Engineering in Middletown became the only Seagram holdings in Kentucky. Over time, even Corporate Engineering would be dissolved as well.

Two Mashbills and Five Yeasts

Seagram saw to it that all five of these distilleries used the same two mashbills or cooking menus that were composed of corn, rye and malt, mixed according to either a mixture of 60% corn, 35% rye, 5% malted barley or 75% corn, 20% rye and 5% malted barley. Seagram only used one yeast strain at these five distilleries. Over time, the other four yeasts became available to all distilleries. This enabled these five production facilities to turn out approximately the same 10 Bourbons that are now only made at the Four Roses Distillery in Lawrenceburg. This was a proprietary designation granted by the contract of sale between Diageo and Kirin in 2002. These five yeast strains and the two mashbills are solely the property of Four Roses and cannot be duplicated by competing distilleries. No other distillery today makes 10 Bourbon recipes in this manner. What makes Four Roses unique as a brand is the result of the Seagram network of distilleries – now there's a fortunate twist of fate.

The Lotus Warehouses

The Lotus Warehouse property, today known as the Four Roses Warehouse & Bottling Facility at Cox's Creek, was comprised of 298 acres with 21 warehouses from "A" to "U" that were completed by December 18, 1960. One warehouse, "O," was torn down in 1992 due to construction defects which made it impractical to use for barrel storage.

Single-story warehouses provide more even aging.

Each warehouse was situated on approximately one acre of land and constructed out of wood cleared from the property. The ground was made to gently slope away from each in such a way that a fire in one would not readily spread to another. Today they are all equipped with sprinklers in the event that a fire should occur. The water source for the sprinkler system comes from a lake with its own pump house on the property.

All of the warehouses are one story high which provides for more even aging since the temperature varies roughly 8 degrees Fahrenheit from the top rack to the bottom one. Traditional metal-clad warehouses in Kentucky will vary as much as 35 degrees Fahrenheit from the bottom to top floors, which will cause a variety of results, including higher evaporation and quicker color retention on top floors and slower results on the lower ones.

Tank trucks of approved distillate are unloaded, then proofed and gauged prior to preparation for barreling.

The bottling operation is capable of producing 300 cases per day from aged whiskeys that are dumped, proofed and gauged in the Regauge area. The whiskey is then cut to bottling proof and chill-filtered, ready to go to the bottling line. Approved barrel-strength whiskey is not cut and isn't chill-filtered. Bulk shipments to customers also originate at this location. This central facility was like a hub of a wheel for all the small Seagram distilleries to send daily loads of approved distillate for barreling when they were in operation.

Today, with an optimum working capacity of 380,000 barrels or less and a bottling facility, Four Roses at Cox's Creek, with its unique single floor barrel storage area, continues to extend very important services contributing to the development of color, aroma and taste of all Four Roses Kentucky Straight Bourbon Whiskeys.

Winds of Change

In an article from the *Beverage Executive* March 15, 1966 edition entitled: "THE SEAGRAM SAGA: IV another Rose, a Bottle and a Fast Dark Horse," the following observations were made.

"Four Roses (along with Paul Jones and Old Baker) had been acquired originally in the fall of 1943 with the Seagram purchase of Frankfort Distillers, Inc. At the time they were acquired, they were 90 proof blends (45%) of straight whiskeys. In 1947, according to Jack Wishny, "Sam (Bronfman) took Four Roses as a blend of straights and converted it to a spirits blend as part of the Bronfman philosophy."

Four Roses always had been a respected name among brands, since long before Prohibition. But under the ministrations of Mr. Sam…the synonym for Four Roses became Go-Go-Go. Early in the war, it was producing 325,000 cases annually; in 1945, it produced 600,000 cases; by 1952, its apparent high spot, it was producing an annual volume of 1,200,000 cases.

In 1952, when the brand was at its sales zenith, *Spirits* magazine did a feature story on Four Roses. At that time, the brand was first in its price class, with a volume "twice that of any runner- up at or above its price." And, "it was one of the best-known, most admired brands in America." *Spirits* reported that Four Roses "has become one of the commercial world's great names" and that it was "at the top of the list on name-a-brand street polls." During this period, whiskey from Indiana made its way into the formula for Four Roses blended whiskey in the United States. Quite a change indeed.

This is the best way we could think of to suggest to you how downright cool and refreshing a whiskey-and-ice-and-soda can be on a warm midsummer afternoon—what matchless flavor and smoothness will be yours to enjoy—*if the whiskey you use is Four Roses!* Just try it and see!

Four Roses is a blend of straight whiskies—90 proof. The straight whiskies in Four Roses are 4 years or more old. Frankfort Distilleries, Incorporated, Louisville and Baltimore.

1940 Ad

The Cake of Ice Ad

"Even today (1966), people recall and associate Four Roses with that classic summer ad which showed four red roses embedded in a cake of ice." What follows is an excerpt from a Four Roses archives copy of a reply written by William R. Wright of Young & Rubicam Advertising to Mr. Bradley Houghton of Four Roses Distillers Company, dated May 17, 1957, about this popular ad that ran for several years in major magazines in the United States.

"The following article appeared in the publication, *100 Top Copy Writers and their Favorite Ads,* produced in 1954 by Printer's Ink.

"The idea for this ad was born on the Merritt Parkway somewhere east of Exit 40 on a late autumn night in 1939. We were driving home from the theater.

For more days than I care to admit, I had been trying to come up with an idea for an August ad reminding readers that a Four Roses highball was something rather special in the way of a cool warm-weather drink. I hadn't been able to hit upon anything I was willing to settle for. Driving along the parkway, the problem kept going through my mind.

'Ice...Four Roses...Four Roses Ice.'

'Hey," I nudged my wife, dozing on the front seat beside me. 'What would you think of freezing four roses in a cake of ice?'

'Sounds sort of crazy to me," she mumbled sleepily.

It was mid-January when Anton Bruehl (a Young & Rubicam photographer) started work on the photograph. Laden with roses, he taxied to the Knickerbocker Ice Company. Four roses were placed in each of the water-filled forms to be frozen. Thin wires, weighted with sinkers, kept the bouquets from floating to the surface.

The next day, nine 300-pound blocks of ice were delivered to Anton's studio. In each block of ice were four roses that looked like a debutante's corsage the morning after. The pressure of the freezing ice had squashed the flowers into a pulpy mass.

'These won't do at all,' Anton said to the iceman. 'Please take them back and try again.' 'Nothing doing,' the iceman said. 'We deliver ice – we don't take it back.'

So Anton and his men lugged the huge ice cakes up to the roof to get them out of the way. The next day, and the next, the same thing happened. The building management complained. For three days the thermometer had hovered in the 20s. The weight of the ice on the roof was approaching the danger point.

Several tons of ice later, it occurred to someone to stop freezing the ice before the center of the block had become solid. The frozen block was then 'cropped' at top and bottom with an ice saw ..."

The ad, with minor modifications, has run almost every year since it first appeared and has been merchandised by the trade to a fare-thee-well. Ice companies all over the United States were told the simple trick of freezing four roses in ice. One year, I remember, actual Four Roses cakes of ice appeared in more than 12,000 retail outlets at the time the ad appeared in the magazines.

Maybe the cake of ice will melt this year, or next. But it will always be my favorite ad. For, more than any other ad for which I have ever been responsible, it re-emphasizes the simple verity that a copy writer's jog involves something more than fine-feathered words –an idea!"

- Henry Lent.

Very special delivery. When you serve a drink made with Four Roses, you really deliver something extra-special. Four Roses, you see, has <u>one</u> quality to be found in no other whiskey—<u>the distinctive flavor</u> that has made this brand the first choice of millions.

Wouldn't <u>you</u> rather drink

Four Roses

Frankfort Distillers Corporation, New York. Blended whiskey. 86.8 proof. 60% grain neutral spirits.

1953 Ad

America's Most Famous Bouquet

A 1950s article in *Modern Packaging* leads off with a popular Four Roses copy line of the time:

"An advertisement millions have seen asks the question:

'Wouldn't you rather drink Four Roses?'

Wouldn't you rather see Four Roses? is just as much to the point so far as packaging is concerned. …Its famous rose spray is a natural for eye appeal, the colors alive with charm. The trademark, of course, gives rise to the powerful, double-edged merchandising theme, 'America's Most Famous Bouquet.'"

The article further states that "In whiskey, more certainly than almost any other field, consistent quality of product is first and most critical. And millions of Americans will back up the maker's proud boast in current advertising that Four Roses is whiskey of the very finest flavor and quality. Its reputation is unsurpassed by any other brand on the market…"

"As a result of the unique name and trademark, …Four Roses is today (1950) one of America's best known trade names, ranking well up with such other famous 'handles' as Coca-Cola, Ford, Jell-O and Kodak."

1936 Ad

1939 Ad

Sorry, the Postman says "No!"

WE WISH we could mail you a Four Roses Hot Toddy—just to let you know what a downright marvelous cold-weather drink it is.

We can't. So we suggest the next best thing:

If you haven't a bottle of Four Roses on hand, get one at the nearest liquor store and follow our recipe for the world's finest hot toddy.

Then settle back in your favorite chair before the fire and slowly sip the warm and fragrant master-piece that you and Four Roses have created!

Recipe for
the world's finest Hot Toddy

Put a piece of sugar in the bottom of a glass and dissolve it with a little hot water. Add a twist of lemon peel (bruise it firmly)...four cloves and, if you desire, a stick of cinnamon. Pour in a generous jigger of that matchless whiskey, Four Roses...and fill the glass with steaming hot water.

Frankfort Distilleries, Inc., Louisville & Baltimore.

FOUR ROSES

A blend of straight whiskies—90 proof

Great Arctic Discovery

IF YOU'VE EVER SIPPED a tall, iced Four-Roses-and-soda on a summer's day, then you know how superbly cool and refreshing it can be.

And if you haven't — well, we believe there's no time like today to make this great arctic discovery for yourself.

Once you do, we're sure you'll agree that Four Roses is a really magnificent whiskey ... mellow, full-bodied, and quite matchless in flavor. It's a whiskey, you'll find, that imparts a particular excellence to your highball. Why not mix yourself a Four-Roses-and-soda ... and see?

FOUR ROSES

A TRULY GREAT WHISKEY

Four Roses is a blend of straight whiskies — 90 proof. Frankfort Distillers Corporation, New York City.

How to make a Sphinx talk

Among your friends there is probably a quiet, reserved fellow who's practically a sphinx when it comes to praising anything.

Well, next time he drops in, serve him a highball made with Four Roses.

We sincerely believe that after the first sip, the "sphinx" will speak right up and say that he's never tasted a whiskey like Four Roses.

That's because Four Roses is an exclusive combination of specially distilled whiskies, selected to achieve a smooth, mellow *distinctively different* flavor.

Nor has the quality of Four Roses been changed. It is still the same great whiskey it was before the war.

FOUR ROSES

The same great whiskey today as before the war

* * *

A blend of straight whiskies—90 proof. Frankfort Distillers Corporation, New York City.

1945 Ad

How to meet a good friend

The information booth at the railway station is a traditional meeting place for friends.

But it's much more likely that you'll be meeting *this* particular friend in your home, or at your favorite bar.

For we're talking about an Old Fashioned made with that matchless whiskey, Four Roses. And Four Roses, as everybody knows, makes the most magnificent Old Fashioned you've ever tasted.

That's why you're in for something extra special every time you say to your barman, "Make mine with Four Roses!"

Four Roses is now a **Blended Whiskey** —a fine blend of 40% straight whiskies, 5 years or more old, and 60% grain neutral spirits. 93.5 proof.

FOUR ROSES

AMERICA'S MOST FAMOUS BOUQUET

Frankfort Distillers Corporation, New York City

1946 Ad

Greater Manhattan

We're talking about the cocktail this time, not the city.

For any way you look at it, a Manhattan *is* greater when it's made with that glorious whiskey —Four Roses.

Four Roses, you see, imparts to any drink a magnificent and truly distinctive flavor. For the whiskey itself is distinctive . . . with a superb taste and grand mellow smoothness all its own.

Next time you make a Manhattan or order one at your favorite bar, be sure that the whiskey is Four Roses. After your first sip, we're sure you'll share our view of this matchless drink.

Fine Blended Whiskey — 90.5 proof. 40% straight whiskies; 60% grain neutral spirits.

Frankfort Distillers Corp., New York.

FOUR ROSES

AMERICA'S MOST FAMOUS BOUQUET

1948 Ad

This will be music to your ears

If you appreciate good whiskey and good value, here are two facts that are well worth listening to:

* Four Roses is a whiskey of the very *finest* flavor and quality.

* Its *reputation* is unsurpassed by any other brand on the market —even brands costing considerably more than Four Roses.

No wonder Four Roses outsells every other whiskey at or above its price—and most other whiskies at any price.

Wouldn't *you* rather drink **FOUR ROSES**

Frankfort Distillers Corporation, N. Y. C. Blended whiskey. 90.5 proof. 60% grain neutral spirits.

1950 Ad

1955 Ad

1956 Ad

1959 Ad

The Four Roses Society

Did you know that there was a Four Roses Society in the late 1950s and early '60s that was featured in many of the Four Roses magazine ads? Seagram even went so far as to market some 33⅓ long-playing, high-fidelity record albums specially pressed by Columbia Record Productions and RCA Victor Custom Records. The titles that we know about included: "Four Roses Dance Party," "Sing with the Four Roses Society" and "Join the Four Roses Song Fest Vol. II." We don't know how many members were included in it or if it hit the top of the charts for specially-produced records at that time.

Enjoy the Good Life
with Four Roses

First sip is whisper-light. Last sip keeps its warmhearted flavor, even in melting ice. Always mixes better. All because it's better than any other whiskey. Only pennies more.

©1961 FOUR ROSES DIST. CO., N.Y.C. • BLENDED WHISKEY • 86 PROOF • 60% GRAIN NEUTRAL SPIRITS.

FOUR ROSES Blended Whisky

1961 Ad

1957 Ad

1961 Ad

1963 Ad

1968 Ad

"UNDERWHELM ME...AGAIN."

IT'S WHISKEY WITHOUT THE WHELM

Smooth, satisfying... but *never* overpowering. Four Roses Premium is a different whiskey. American Light Whiskey. Let it underwhelm you.

FOUR ROSES
PREMIUM

AMERICAN LIGHT WHISKEY · A BLEND · 100% AMERICAN WHISKEY · 86 PROOF · © 1973 FOUR ROSES DIST. CO. N.Y.C.

1973 Ad

CHAPTER SIX:

A Brand in Decline, Goodbye to America! 1971 – 2000

Frankfort in Decline

A half-dozen years from the time the glowing article in *Modern Packaging* was written, it was noted by Seagram management that, in 1956, the name of Frankfort Distillers Sales Company should be changed to Four Roses Distillers Company because "Four Roses had become one of the most respected trademarks," while Frankfort had less meaning to the general public.

A Change in Taste

With Four Roses blended whiskey sales slowly declining, the Joseph E. Seagram & Sons, Inc., domestic sales company in charge of the brand, determined that the primary reason was a gradual change in the taste preference of American consumers. It was also apparent to the company that no amount of advertising expenditure or sales effort could halt the downward trend and that a total change in the product and the package was necessary.

Citing the spectacular gains of imported whiskeys and white goods over previous years, Seagram executives indicated that it was their view that "the American Consumer has been demonstrating that he prefers a light-bodied, more versatile drink."

Light Whiskey

They further stated that, in their estimation, the consumer no longer wanted to belly up to the bar, take a belt and feel it in his toes. In their opinion, the drinkers of that day wanted a light product in the new category of "Light Whiskey."

The advent of "Light Whiskey" during the 1960s allowed U.S. distillers to reduce costs by distilling at a higher proof and to age in either used charred barrels or new un-charred barrels. In 1968, federal regulations were changed so that this new product identity could compete with popular Scotch and Canadian whiskies. Thus the law was changed in January of 1968 and put into effect by July 1, 1972.

There were contests and legal arguments about it but, in the end, they won their products the right to be designated "Light Whiskey" without derogatory labeling requirements. This resulted in the government's recognizing that very light distillates aged in seasoned charred barrels were actually whiskey, the same as in Canada and Scotland.

Soon after, a completely new product was introduced – Four Roses Premium American Light Whiskey – which, they claimed, was America's highest-selling light whiskey at the time. With this in mind, these same executives pointed out that a new product, Four Roses Premium, introduced early in 1971, delivered the taste of Light Whiskey a year earlier.

Claims were made that they had developed a totally new product in Four Roses Premium and presented the fact that the specially aged grain spirits in the brand were to be replaced by Light Whiskey distilled at a fractionally lower proof. They further claimed that the taste would be identical and that Four Roses Premium had already earned solid consumer acceptance.

Sink or Swim!

Money for Four Roses advertising stopped flowing and the domestic blended whiskey was allowed to languish, pushing the once most widely known and venerated name in American whiskey down to a lower position on retailer's shelves. It soon got to the point that some would not even carry it at all.

Over There!

The Four Roses Kentucky Straight Bourbon Whiskey brand was thriving overseas when Seagram and Kirin established The Kirin-Seagram Co., Ltd. in 1972 for marketing and distribution in Japan.

In the export market, SOSSCO (Seagram Overseas Sales Company) was doing a land office business with the yellow label version. With working partnerships involving Chivas Brothers in Scotland and a facility in Germany, the Four Roses label was gaining market share throughout Europe. The partnership with Kirin was also reaping sizeable rewards for Seagram in Japan as well.

A Change in Leadership

It was almost a self-fulfilling prophecy that had been foretold by Mr. Sam when, before his death, he was heard to say the old expression, "Shirtsleeves to shirtsleeves in three generations." Simply stated, it meant that the first generation rolls up its sleeves and makes the business successful, the second one maintains it and the third one rolls them up and succeeds in tearing down what the second had tried to manage. It summed up what was to be the fate of the Bronfman family's leadership of Joseph E. Seagram & Sons, Inc.

Well, you see, after Mr. Sam's death in July, 1977, the talented management at Seagram was led by his son Edgar in the United States at 375 Park Avenue in New York, and his other son Charles, in charge of the company's Canadian interests in Montreal.

Above: Four Roses Yellow thrived in Europe and Japan.

In an attempt to be "leaner" under this new leadership, the corporation went through a series of upheavals resulting in the sale of many of the time-honored brands that had made the corporation so successful for so long. As a result, these brands were eagerly purchased by competitors who either milked them for what little they were worth or retired them to stave off the fears of competition in a highly competitive industry.

An Uncertain Future

All of this and the future of Four Roses Bourbon were significantly impacted when, in the 1990s, Edgar put his son Edgar, Jr. in charge of the company. With little practical knowledge of the business, Edgar, Jr. was soon interested in taking the company into businesses foreign to the core structure of the Seagram Corporation: music and entertainment.

In 1999, the Corporation's wine and spirits assets merged with Vivendi to form Vivendi Universal. Under the guidance of Jacques Missioner, it was soon obvious to those who knew about the beverage alcohol business that Vivendi's leadership was doomed.

Rutledge in Kentucky

"The Master Distiller" sounds like an awfully important title for someone to carry for a very good reason – it is. To achieve this lofty status at a distillery, one must be able to wear a lot of distinctly different hats. One has to be a good salesman. A teacher. A chemist. An ambassador. A connoisseur. An artist. A spokesman. A marketer. A public speaker. A storyteller. A historian. A politician. A team player. A leader. A diplomat. A visionary. And the truly legendary Master Distillers are the ones who wear every one of these hats with an easy, comfortable grace, as well as with a relaxed style and humility that sets them apart from all the rest.

Since 1995, and even now, after his retirement on September 1, 2015, Four Roses has enjoyed a remarkably passionate relationship with one of the legendary Master Distillers of our time, Jim Rutledge.

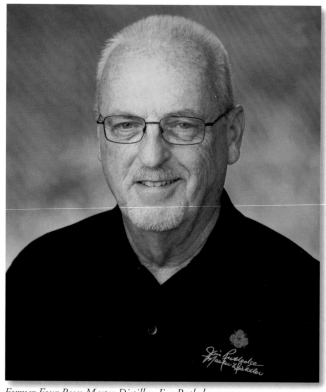

Former Four Roses Master Distiller, Jim Rutledge

To give you some idea of the respect the man enjoys among his peers, in a move that surprised no one, except for maybe Jim, he was named to the inaugural class of the Bourbon Hall of Fame.

It is not an exaggeration by any stretch of the imagination to say that without Jim Rutledge, there would not be all of the different, distinct and exquisite Bourbons produced by Four Roses, but also – there would probably not even be any Four Roses to enjoy in America at all. For Jim, almost single-handidly, with a dogged persistence that Lawrence Lavalle Jones himself might have envied, is solely responsible for the return of the Four Roses brand to this country.

His story with the brand begins back in 1966, when Jim Rutledge started out with Seagram in Research and Development at the Louisville plant. His intelligence and passion for doing a great job marked him for success from the very start.

In the following years, whether it was in the research department, at the distillery, in bottling, finished goods, warehousing or industrial engineering, Jim showed his ability to handle any and all responsibilities thrown his way as he climbed the Seagram corporate ladder.

When he was transferred to the corporate office in New York in 1975 as the head of industrial engineering and budgets, Jim was as close as it gets to the leadership of the corporation. He stayed at this office for 17 years.

It was during these years that Jim's passion for Four Roses began to stir. From his vantage point in New York, he could see that this brand needed a lot more care and attention than it was being given in its production and quality.

So, in 1992, Jim asked to return to his home state of Kentucky to help with the Four Roses brand. Soon after, Jim went to Cox's Creek to oversee the budgets and, in November of 1994, he took over the position of Master Distiller from Ova Haney.

Almost immediately after his return to Kentucky, Jim began his quest to bring the brand back to Kentucky and the United States. Time and time again, he pleaded his case with the people he knew in the corporate offices in New York. Nearly every conversation between Jim and New York would include an argument, or rationale, as to why the brand should return. His tenacity quickly earned him the name "Mr. Four Roses" by those in New York who regularly took Jim's phone calls.

Finally, at the end of 1994, Jim convinced the company to allow Four Roses 80 Proof Yellow to be made available on a limited basis in Kentucky so that at the very least, the people at the distillery who made it every day were finally able to buy it. Without any advertising or support, the brand found its way to retail shelves in Kentucky for the undervalued price of $9.95 a bottle.

This, of course, was just the start for Jim. His determination, energy and drive brought the Four Roses brand back to America on a grand scale. But it was truly his passion above all that made a real difference in the success of the brand, both here and around the world.

Award-Winning Master Distiller

Jim Rutledge was named the Master Distiller at Four Roses Distillery in 1995. As a member of the inaugural class of the Bourbon Hall of Fame, Jim was also inducted into Whisky Magazine's *Hall of Fame in 2013.*

In 2007, Malt Advocate *magazine awarded Jim the "Lifetime Achievement Award." In 2008, they named Four Roses Distillery "Distillery of the Year." Also, in 2008, Four Roses Distillery was named* Whisky Magazine's *"Innovator of the Year" during the magazine's annual Icons of Whisky Awards and they named Jim the industry's American Whiskey "2008 Ambassador of the Year." The magazine has also named Four Roses Distillery "Distiller of the Year" three consecutive years for 2011, 2012 and 2013.*

After 49 years with the company, Jim retired from his position as Master Distiller on September 1, 2015.

The First Kentucky Bourbon Festival Four Roses Tasting

"As I remember it, we had to get special permission to bring Four Roses Yellow into Kentucky for this event. Once that was secured, Mike Bullock (Distillery Key Supervisor at the time) and I bought a piece of rug to put under a borrowed card table on which we placed a tablecloth, a pot with a dozen roses, some cups and some Four Roses Yellow.

After the opening ceremony, it was all Ova Haney, Jim Rutledge, Mike Bullock and I could do to give out samples to everyone. When local and visiting Japanese guests arrived, they kept yelling "Four Roses" as they literally ran to our table." - Al Young

Chapter Seven:

Back and Better Than Ever. 2000 – Present

For several months after the sale to Vivendi, apprehensions and concerns were plentiful as to whether Four Roses would survive as either a company or as a label with the product made somewhere else – or, worst of all, a closed distillery with nothing at all. Even with a good sense of viability in the export market, the lack of a domestic presence for the once stellar old brand was very troublesome.

Almost as soon as the new partnership was completed, a sell-off was in the making. Diageo and Pernod Ricard, the two largest alcohol companies in the world at the time, established a consortium and decided to buy the Four Roses business. Private investment groups were also formed but were unable to raise sufficient funds to even be considered as serious bidders.

A New Beginning!

Kirin Acquires Global Business of Four Roses

In February 2002, Kirin acquired the worldwide business of the Four Roses brand of Kentucky Bourbon. A company has been established as a subsidiary of Kirin Holdings America in the United States to handle the rights to Four Roses, including a distillery. Acquisition of this major Bourbon brand has strengthened Kirin's spirits business.

Four Roses is Kentucky Straight Bourbon with a hearty bouquet and mild taste that is a leading brand, familiar to consumers around the world. Besides Japan, it is sold in France, Spain and other countries throughout the world.

Today, Kirin is the parent company for Four Roses Bourbon. The scope of this ownership has allowed everything in Lawrenceburg and Cox's Creek to remain intact.

As soon as Kirin established a new shape of Four Roses business in 2001, Mr. Yoshio Enomoto became the first president and decided to move the company's headquarter functions to Tokyo.

The days of the blended whiskey version are long past. An effort was made to buy up and remove as much of it as possible from the domestic market. No longer should there be any confusion about the fact that Four Roses stands for 100% Kentucky Straight Bourbon Whiskey – nothing less.

In 2002, when Four Roses started its business with a new shape, Teruyuki Daino was assigned as President and CEO, succeeding Yoshio Enomoto. It was his strategy to introduce Four Roses nationwide. Working with Master Distiller Jim Rutledge and Director of Quality/Product Planning, Jota Tanaka, Daino launched two new Four Roses products to the U.S. and Europe: Four Roses Single Barrel and Four Roses Small Batch. He also introduced a new label for Four Roses Yellow to the U.S. and Europe. Then, in 2005, he transferred the headquarter functions back to

Lawrenceburg, Kentucky. Mr. Daino successfully established the fundamentals of the current business model, while laying the groundwork for the current branding initiatives.

The Japanese market, meanwhile, has grown to become the largest market in sales volume for Four Roses worldwide. In 2002, Kirin and Seagram discontinued their joint venture, Kirin-Seagram. Kirin now imports, markets, distributes and sells Four Roses in Japan.

In Europe, Mr. Marek Holub was named General Manager Four Roses Europe, Kirin Europe GmbH in 2002. Since then, he has expanded Four Roses into more than 30 countries.

In 2009, Mr. Daino returned to Japan after seven successful years at the head of Four Roses and was succeeded by Mr. Hideki Horiguchi. Mr. Horiguchi continued the strategy established by Mr. Daino, while expanding Four Roses into all 50 states in the U.S., and was involved with new and renewed markets in Europe and The Middle East until returning to Japan in 2013.

Mr. Taiji Abe came to Four Roses in 2013. During his brief stay in Kentucky, an additional Visitor's Center and Barrel Tasting room were completed at our Cox's Creek Warehouse and Bottling facility. Also, further plans for production expansion at both locations began to take shape under his administration. In April of 2015, Taiji (as he preferred to be called) returned to Kirin in Japan.

During the spring of 2015, Ms. Satoko Yoshida came to Four Roses. It is she who will in many ways lead the brand forward as expansion plans are implemented at the Distillery and the Cox's Creek Warehouse and Bottling facility over the next several years.

The return of marketing to America

In 2004, Yellow Label was on the retail shelves in Kentucky and Four Roses and Kirin were about to introduce a new brand to America – Four Roses Single Barrel Bourbon. It was time to get serious about marketing once again.

One of the new concepts in the U.S. was that the Four Roses brand should be synonymous with the term "mellow." It only takes one sip to understand why this direction was chosen with little discussion or argument.

The next decision was an equally important one. The team agreed that the reputation the brand earned during the "blended spirits" years still lingered and was something that needed to be addressed and overcome as quickly as possible. It was then decided to stop all marketing of the Yellow Label brand and to market only the premium Four Roses Single Barrel product in an effort to position the brand as a high-end, high quality Bourbon. (It was a good thing when *Whisky Magazine* named Single Barrel the "Best American Whiskey Under 10 Years Old" at the Best of the Best Awards of 2005.)

So with the direction chosen it was then decided to creatively use the iconic imagery of a red rose in all advertising and marketing materials, while communicating the messages of smooth and mellow at all times. And just like that, a long-term marketing campaign was born.

FOUR ROSES | MADE IN AMERICA SINCE 1888

L'ABUS D'ALCOOL EST DANGEREUX POUR LA SANTÉ. À CONSOMMER AVEC MODÉRATION

2004 European Ad

2008 European Ad

2011 Japanese Ad

No thorns.

Four Roses Single Barrel
Kentucky Straight Bourbon Whiskey

Outdoor, 2005

Sequential Outdoor, 2005

Outdoor, 2007

Outdoor, 2007

Outdoor, July 2014

Outdoor, November 2014

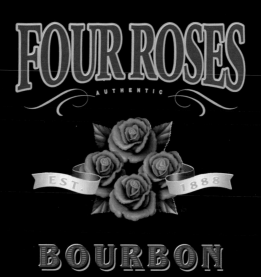

Above at Top: Early Four Roses Bourbon Logo.   Above: Current Redesigned Four Roses Bourbon Logo

CHAPTER EIGHT:

Our Bourbons

Four Roses is the only distillery that uses two mashbills and five proprietary yeast strains to produce 10 distinct Bourbon recipes. Each of these 10 Bourbon recipes has its own unique recipe. Here's how it works.

Every Bourbon recipe has four letter designations. The first letter and third letter are constants with the only two variables being the mashbill and the yeast strain.

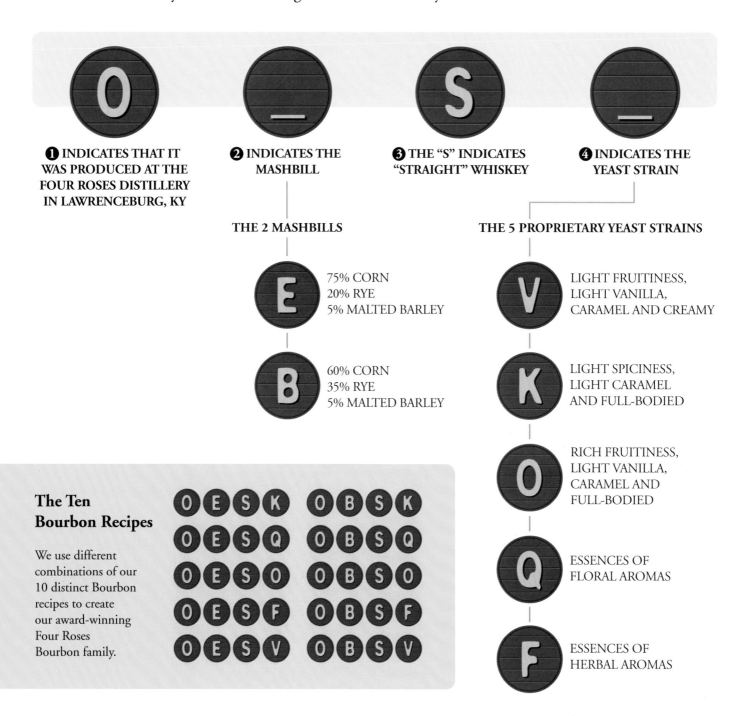

❶ INDICATES THAT IT WAS PRODUCED AT THE FOUR ROSES DISTILLERY IN LAWRENCEBURG, KY

❷ INDICATES THE MASHBILL

❸ THE "S" INDICATES "STRAIGHT" WHISKEY

❹ INDICATES THE YEAST STRAIN

THE 2 MASHBILLS

E — 75% CORN / 20% RYE / 5% MALTED BARLEY

B — 60% CORN / 35% RYE / 5% MALTED BARLEY

THE 5 PROPRIETARY YEAST STRAINS

V — LIGHT FRUITINESS, LIGHT VANILLA, CARAMEL AND CREAMY

K — LIGHT SPICINESS, LIGHT CARAMEL AND FULL-BODIED

O — RICH FRUITINESS, LIGHT VANILLA, CARAMEL AND FULL-BODIED

Q — ESSENCES OF FLORAL AROMAS

F — ESSENCES OF HERBAL AROMAS

The Ten Bourbon Recipes

We use different combinations of our 10 distinct Bourbon recipes to create our award-winning Four Roses Bourbon family.

O E S K   O B S K
O E S Q   O B S Q
O E S O   O B S O
O E S F   O B S F
O E S V   O B S V

Single Barrel – A New Flagship

In 2004, Four Roses Single Barrel was introduced in Kentucky. It quickly became the leading seller of its type and earned both critical acclaim and major industry awards.

Four Roses Single Barrel Awards

Double Gold
- *Denver International Spirits Competition 2014*

Number 1 Bourbon
- *F. Paul Pacult's* Spirits Journal 2009

Gold Medal
- *San Francisco World Spirits Competition 2008, 2009, 2010, 2012*

Best Buy: 96 -100 Points
- *Wine Enthusiast 2010*

Ultimate Recommendation: 95 Points
- *Ultimate Spirits Challenge 2012*

Single Barrel Recipe:

A Passion for Innovation – Small Batch and Limited Editions

In 2006, our Small Batch Bourbon premiered.

Four Roses Small Batch Awards

Double Gold
- *San Francisco World Spirits Competition 2015*

Gold Medal
- *San Francisco World Spirits Competition 2008, 2010, 2014*

Gold
- *Denver International Spirits Competition 2014*

Best Bourbon No Age
- Whisky Magazine *World Whiskies Awards 2009*

Best Buy: 96 - 100 Points
- *Wine Enthusiast 2010*

Highly Recommended: 94 Points
- *Ultimate Spirits Challenge 2012*

Best American Whiskey, Bourbon 7 Years & under
- Whisky Magazine *World Whiskies Awards 2012*

Small Batch Recipes:

O B S K
O E S K
O B S O
O E S O

Limited Editions

Every year, our Master Distiller selects a few barrels of exceptional Bourbons from our warehouses to become Four Roses Limited Edition Releases. It began in 2007 with the release of a very special Four Roses Limited Edition Single Barrel in commemoration of Master Distiller Jim Rutledge's 40th year in the distilling industry. The Mariage collection of Small Batch was initiated in 2008 and renamed as the "Small Batch Limited Edition" in 2010. In 2009, the Four Roses Private Barrel Program was established to allow a few of our retailers to come in for a private tasing and selection, which we then private labeled for our retailers to offer to their customers.

Four Roses Limited Edition Awards
Double Gold
- *San Francisco World Spirits Competiton 2014*

#1 The 15 Best New Spirits of 2013, Four Roses Limited Edition Single Barrel 2013
- *Paste Magazine*

Four Roses Limited Edition Single Barrel 2011 Release Four Star/Highly Recommended
- *F. Paul Pacult's* Spirit Journal, *June Issue*

#3 out of 140 Best Five Star Spirits in the World 2012 – Four Roses Limited Edition 2012
- *F. Paul Pacult's* Spirit Journal, *June Issue*

Four Roses Mariage
Double Gold Mariage Collection 2008
- *San Francisco World Spirits Competition 2008*

Four Roses Mariage Collection 2008 Release Five Star Rating Highest Recommendation
- *F. Paul Pacult's* Spirit Journal

Bronze – Packaging Design Mariage Collection
- *San Francisco World Spirits Competition 2008*

#52 out of 115 Best Five Star Spirits 2009 – Four Roses Mariage Collection 2008 Release
- *F. Paul Pacult's* Spirit Journal

Mariage Collection 2009, Gold Medal 94 Points "Exceptional"
- *Beverage Testing Institute: The 2010 International Review of Spirits*

Four Roses Limited Edition Small Batch
American Whiskey of the Year 2013
- Whisky Advocate, *2013 Winter Issue*

2012 Four Roses Limited Edition Small Batch: 94 Points
- *Ultimate Spirits Challenge 2012*

2012 Four Roses Limited Edition Small Batch: 96 Points #1 Whisky
- Whisky Advocate, *2012 Winter Issue*

American Whiskey of the Year 2012
- Whisky Advocate, *2013 Spring Issue*

Four Roses Private Barrel Program
Single Barrel: Barrel Strength
Double Gold
- *San Francisco World Spirits Competition 2014*

Gold Medal, 93 Points, "Exceptional"
- *Beverage Testing Institute: The 2010 International Review of Spirits*

Gold Medal
- *San Francisco World Spirits Competition 2010*

Strong Recommendation: 89 Points OBSQ Recipe
- *Ultimate Spirits Challenge 2010*

Excellent/Highly Recommended: 91 Points OESQ Recipe
- *Ultimate Spirits Challenge 2010*

Yellow

And through it all, the widely acclaimed and award-winning 80 proof Four Roses Kentucky Straight Bourbon captured the tastes and hearts of those who have grown to love it in Europe, Japan and the United States.

Four Roses Yellow Awards

Gold Medal
- *San Francisco World Spirits Competition 2014*

Gold
- *Denver International Spirits Competition 2014*

Top 50 Spirits Award 2013
- Wine Enthusiast Magazine

World Whiskey Awards 2010
- *American Whiskey Best Bourbon 7 Years and Under*

Excellent/Highly Recommended 92 Points
- *Ultimate Spirits Challenge 2010*

Silver Medal
- *San Francisco World Spirits Competition 2010*

Yellow Recipe: Uses up to all 10 Bourbon recipes.

U.S. Bottle   *European Bottle*

Distillery of the Year Four Roses
- Malt Advocate *Whiskey Award 2008*

Whisky Distiller of the Year 2011, 2012, 2013 & 2015
- *Icons of Whisky America,* Whisky Magazine

Innovator of the Year 2008
- *Icons of Whisky America,* Whisky Magazine

Four Roses Black
This fine old Bourbon offers a rich, robust and full-bodied flavor with a delicate touch of spiciness. Sold only in Japan. 80 proof (40%).

Four Roses Super Premium
This small batch Bourbon is often referred to as "Platinum" for the elegance of its rich and complex taste. Introduced in 1992. Sold only in Japan. 86 proof (43%).

Black Recipes: OBSK, OESK
Super Premium Recipes: OBSK, OESK, OBSV, OESV

A New Master Distiller Continues the Tradition

A native of Owensboro, Kentucky, Brent Elliott became Master Distiller at Four Roses Bourbon in September 2015. He is uniquely qualified for this new role as he's been practicing the craft of making Four Roses Bourbon since 2005, working closely with former Master Distiller, Jim Rutledge.

As the Distillery's Director of Quality for nearly a decade, Brent's experience has included everything from evaluating Bourbons in the tasting lab, to taking part in selecting barrels for Single Barrel, Limited Edition and Private Barrel Program products. In the years ahead, Brent's dedication and passion will ensure that each Four Roses product has the fruity, smooth and mellow character, along with a hint of spice, that the brand has become know for around the world.

Or, as explained in Brent's own words, "My job will be to make sure everything that goes into every bottle is as good as it was yesterday, as good as it has been in the past."

The Distillery Continues to Grow

The Distillery in Transition

In 1983, C. Beam, the distillery plant manager, was replaced by O.O. Haney, who was interested in restoring the building to its former appearance after many years of neglect by Seagram upper management. Segram's only concern was for the distillery to turn out high quality distillate that would then mature into quality Bourbon to be used in Four Roses Bourbon and the blends such as Seven Crown, as well as two prestige blended brands of Canadian Whisky, Crown Royal and Seagram's V.O.

Over the years, a grain bucket elevator had been placed in the front after the hanging roof had been removed. The ornamental iron work that had once secured it was given away with one piece ending up as an ornamental mailbox stand.

The grain storage areas in the ceiling above the main floor had been used to gravity-feed the mills which, in turn, sent grain to either the cooker or the yeast masher. They were problematic in terms of dust and the effect they had on air quality and needed to be replaced.

Using copies of the original blueprints from the Louisville architectural firm of Joseph & Joseph, Seagram's Central Engineering directed the restoration of the exterior of the main distillery building to its original appearance.

With the restoration, exterior grain silos and a mill building were added to improve the air quality and free up some space for dust collectors and meal bins inside the building itself.

With a less than enthusiastic blessing, Seagram finally allowed for the completion and submission of the forms that would result in the building being placed on the National Register of Historic Places in 1987.

Well, the "Old Lady" has gone through a lot of changes since 1910. Computers were added in the 1990s. A walkway above the distillery's main floor was constructed to ensure that visitors could safely move about the distillery to learn more about Four Roses' unique process.

Additional office space was needed, so in 1991, a building was added to house Four Roses' production offices, laboratory, break room, Visitor's Center and gift shop.

In 2004, Four Roses grew again with the addition of more office space in a new building at the top of the hill, not far from where the farm house once stood. An additional building adding even more office space was completed in 2012, allowing Four Roses to convert the office building at the top of the hill into a new gift shop and Visitor's Center.

The year 2015 heralded expansion plans costing $55 million dollars to enhance our production facilities in both locations.

At the Distillery, these plans will entail: more whole grain storage; another cooker; additional yeast tubs; more fermenters; another beer still and doubler; as well as more tanks for finished distillate.

Meanwhile, at Cox's Creek, expansion plans call for: an additional building to house a higher speed bottling line; new offices and processing tanks; as well as more warehouses and increased support equipment.

As you can see, a lot has happened to both the Four Roses brand and to our Kentucky homes over many decades. Perhaps the hope for the future of Four Roses Kentucky Straight Bourbon may be best expressed by the saying on the "Montrose" sundail for 1914. "Grow old with me – the best is yet to be!"

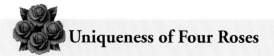 **Uniqueness of Four Roses**

- **High Quality Grain Source**
- **2 Mashbills**
- **10 Different Bourbon Recipes**
- **Single-Story Warehouses**
- **5 Proprietary Yeast Strains**

Four Roses Mashbills

	E Mashbill	**B** Mashbill
Corn	75%	60%
Rye	20%	35%
Malted Barley	5%	5%
	100%	100%

Proprietary Yeasts: V K O Q F   V K O Q F

5 recipes   +   5 recipes

Resulting in **10** distinctive Bourbon recipes that are distilled and aged separately.

Proprietary Yeast Codes

V = Delicate Fruitiness   Q = Floral Essence

K = Slight Spice   F = Herbal

O = Rich Fruitiness

Deciphering Recipe Codes

Four Roses Bourbon uses a recipe code system to identify each of the Bourbons we produce. The first letter, "O" stands for Old Prentice Distillery – the Seagram name for our current Distillery. It remains in the first position regardless of the recipe. Next to it either an "E" or a "B" signifies the mashbill followed by "S" for simple distillation. Finally, the last letter represents one of the proprietary yeasts (V, K, O, Q, F) used to produce a single, unique Four Roses Bourbon.

Four Roses Product Attributes

Four Roses Yellow - 80 Proof
A combination of up to all ten recipes.

Four Roses Small Batch - 90 Proof
A mingling of four of the ten recipes from specially selected barrels in a small batch operation of approximately nineteen barrels.

Four Roses Single Barrel - 100 Proof
It is made from the high rye mashbill with one of the five yeasts then derived from specially selected barrels.

Four Roses Black - 80 Proof
This fine old Bourbon offers a rich, robust and full-bodied flavor with a delicate touch of spiciness. This Bourbon uses several of our Bourbon recipes to achieve its taste profile.

Four Roses Super Premium - 86 Proof
This small batch Bourbon is often referred to as "Platinum" for the elegance of its rich and complex taste. This Bourbon uses several of our Bourbon recipes to achieve its taste profile.

Limited Edition Single Barrel Bourbon (Only in U.S.)

Barrel Strength and non-chill-filtered

2007 – 40th Anniversary / OE Mashbill with O Yeast aged 13.5 years
2008 – 120th / OB Mashbill with K Yeast aged 12 years
2009 – Limited Edition / OE Mashbill with Q yeast aged 10 years
2010 – 100th Anniversary / OB Mashbill with V yeast aged 17 years
2011 – Limited Edition / OB Mashbill with V yeast aged 12 Years
2012 – Limited Edition / OE Mashbill with K yeast aged 12 Years
2013 – Limited Edition / B Mashbill with K yeast aged 13 Years
2014 – Limited Edition / OE Mashbill with F yeast aged 12 Years
2016 – Elliott's Select / OE Mashbill with K yeast aged 14 Years

Limited Edition Small Batch Bourbon (Only in U.S.)

Barrel Strength and non-chill-filtered

Mariage Collection 2008 – September '08
OB Mashbill with V Yeast aged 13 years, 5 months
OE Mashbill with K Yeast aged 10 years, 10 months

Mariage Collection 2009 – September '09
OB Mashbill with K yeast aged 19 years, 10 months
OE Mashbill with O yeast aged 10 years

Limited Edition Small Batch – September '10
OB Mashbill with V yeast aged 15 years
OB Mashbill with K yeast aged 11 years
OE Mashbill with K yeast aged 10 years

Limited Edition Small Batch – September '11
OB Mashbill with K yeast aged 13 years
OE Mashbill with K yeast aged 11 years
OE Mashbill with V yeast aged 12 years
OE Mashbill with Q yeast aged 13 years

Limited Edition Small Batch – September '12
OB Mashbill with V yeast aged 17 years
OB Mashbill with V yeast aged 11 years
OB Mashbill with K yeast aged 12 years
OE Mashbill with K yeast aged 12 years

Limited Edition Small Batch – September '13
OB Mashbill with V yeast aged 18 years
OB Mashbill with K yeast aged 13 years
OE Mashbill with K yeast aged 13 years

Limited Edition Small Batch – September '14
OB Mashbill with K yeast aged 10 years
OE Mashbill with V yeast aged 12 years
OB Mashbill with V yeast aged 14 years
OB Mashbill with F yeast aged 12 years

Limited Edition Small Batch – September '15
OB Mashbill with K yeast aged 16 years
OE Mashbill with K yeast aged 15 years
OE Mashbill with K yeast aged 14 years
OB Mashbill with V yeast aged 11 years

Private Barrel Programs (Only in U.S.)

One of the first of its kind, Four Roses started the program in June of 2007, offering customers the opportunity to choose their own barrel and recipe of Four Roses Bourbon for bottling.

How to connect with us

Four Roses Website
www.FourRosesBourbon.com

Four Roses Facebook
www.facebook.com/fourrosesbourbon

Four Roses Mellow Moments Club in the U.S.
www.mellowmomentsclub.com

Resources

The Four Roses Archive collection consisting of articles, reports, label approvals, magazine ads, photographs and written documents pertaining to the Four Roses brand's ownership under both the Frankfort Distilleries and Joseph. E. Seagram & Sons, Inc. has been used to prepare this document.

Copies of papers and historical documents pertaining to the Jones family were added to the collection courtesy of Dr. Lawrence M. Jones.

Michael Veach, Assistant Archive Curator at the Filson Club and author, provided additional guidance and support during the research phase of this work.

Bibliography

30s All-American Ads. Editor, Jim Heimann. TASCHEN Koln 2003.

Cobb, Irvin S. *Irvin S. Cobb's Own Recipe Book*. Frankfort Distilleries Incorporated of Louisville and Baltimore, Copyright 1936.

Cobb, Irvin S. *Red Likker*. The Copp Clark Co. Publishers, Toronto, Canada, 1929.

Crowgey, Henry G. *Kentucky Bourbon – The Early Years of Whiskeymaking*. Lexington, Kentucky: The University Press of Kentucky, 1971.

Downard, William L. *Dictionary of the History of the American Brewing and Distilling Industries*. Westport, Connecticut: Greenwood Press, 1980.

Faith, Nicholas. *The Bronfmans – The Rise and Fall of the House of Seagram*. St. Martin's Press, New York, New York, 2007.

Hayes, William. *City in Time/ New York*. Sterling Publishing Co., Inc. New York, NY. 2007

Hixson, Kenneth R. *Forty Miles, Forty Bridges – The Story of the Frankfort & Cincinnati Railroad*. Henry Clay Press, Lexington, KY 2007.

Marrus, Michael R. *Samuel Bronfman The Life and Times of Seagram's Mr. Sam*. University Press of New England, Hanover, New Hampshire, 1991.

McCullough, David. *Mornings on Horseback*. Simon & Schuster Paperbacks, New York, New York. 1981-2001

Regan, Gary and Mardee Haidin. *The Book of Bourbon And Other Fine American Whiskeys*. Chapters Publishing Ltd, Shelburne, Vermont, 1995.

Scott, Berkeley and Jeanine. Images of America – The Kentucky Bourbon Trail. Arcadia Publishing, Charleston, South Carolina, et. al. 2009

Scott, Sir Walter. *A Legend of Montrose*. The Echo Library, 2005.

Tell, Darcy. *Times Square Spectacular Lighting Up Broadway*. Harper Collins Publishers, New York, New York 2007

The Kentucky Encyclopedia. Editor in Chief, John E. Kleber. Lexington, Kentucky: The University Press of Kentucky, 1992.

The Encyclopedia of Louisville. Editor in Chief , John E. Kleber. Lexington, Kentucky: The University Press of Kentucky, 2001.

Willkie, H.F. *Beverage Spirits in America – A Brief History*. New York: The Newcomen Society of England, American Branch, 1949.

Image Credit

Courier-Journal/Louisville Times, Paul Jones Jr. (1895), pg.21

Gargala, Nick (2013), pg.72

Getty Images, Pouring out illegal alcohol in the sewer (1921), pg.32

Getty Images, Samuel Bronfman (1966), pg.46

Getty Images, Sailor kissing nurse in Times Square (1945), pg.40

Getty Images, Melly Meadows, pg.24

iStock, Friendly Cow (2009), pg.53

iStock, Distillery Still (2007), pg.18

Jupiter Images, Desk Lamp, pg.45

loc.gov, Alexander Gardner: Lincoln Portrait (1863), pg.17

New York Times, Whisky Plea to Taft (June 20 1909), pg.30

Wikimedia.org, Park and Third Avenue in Louisville (1897), pg.22

Wikimedia.org, Henry Clay (1824), pg.14

Wikimedia.org, William Howard Taft (1908), pg.29

Wikipedia.org, Portrait of Chester A. Arthur (1882), pg.27

Wikipedia.org, Confederate Major General Nathan Bedford Forrest, pg.18

Wikipedia.org, Alice Hathaway Roosevelt (1880), pg.27

Wikipedia.org, Claude Monet (1873), pg.48

Wikipedia.org, American Flag, pg.16

Wikipedia.org, Confederate Flag, pg.16

Wikipedia.org, Vintage Louisville, pg.28

Witzke, Chris (2015), pgs. 37, 74, 77

Photos and Images Courtesy of Dr. Lawrence Jones pgs.15, 25, 31, 37, 45

Photos and Images Courtesy of Four Roses Archives, pgs.
25, 26, 31, 33, 34-36, 39, 41, 42-44, 47, 49, 50-56, 58-63, 65-69, 71, 74-83, 85, 89